NO
MEAT
REQUIRED

NO

THE CULTURAL HISTORY AND CULINARY FUTURE

MEAT

of PLANT-BASED EATING

REQUIRED

ALICIA KENNEDY

Beacon Press ■ Boston

Beacon Press
Boston, Massachusetts
www.beacon.org

Beacon Press books
are published under the auspices of
the Unitarian Universalist Association of Congregations.

27 26 25 24   8 7 6 5 4 3 2 1

This book is printed on acid-free paper that meets the uncoated paper
ANSI/NISO specifications for permanence as revised in 1992.

Text design and composition by Kim Arney

Library of Congress Cataloging-in-Publication Data is available for this title.
ISBN: 978-0-8070-2028-9; e-book: 978-0-8070-6918-9;
audiobook: 978-0-8070-1285-7

To my grandma, Elizabeth,
who taught me how to eat.

To my brother, Brian,
who reminded me.

CONTENTS

INTRODUCTION

This morning I learned how to clean banana blossoms to ready them for cooking. You peel off the thick purple outer leaves to reveal tiny yellow flowers beneath, which are removed and put to the side. Once all the little flowers have been removed, it's time to remove the stamen and calyx from each. These parts are inedible. With the smallest flowers, though, the ones that grow closest to the heart, nothing need be done; there's no stamen or calyx. Once cleaned up, the remaining yellow flowers are put into a bowl of water with the juice of a lime, which keeps them from oxidizing and turning completely brown. Then they get dried off and cooked, maybe into a stir-fry or a curry, perhaps a fritter in a spiced batter. I hadn't listened to my friend from Tamil Nadu, in India, who told me to grease my hands or wear gloves while going through this process, and now my thumbnails are stained black. I've learned a lesson about following instructions.

I'd never cooked or eaten banana blossoms before. They're traditional to South and Southeast Asia, as well as South America—in Costa Rica, a *picadillo de chira de guineo* (*chira de guineo* meaning "banana flower") is eaten with tortillas. Here in Puerto Rico, where I live, I haven't heard of them being used, despite how ubiquitous bananas are both in the terrain and in the cuisine. That we can eat these banana blossoms feels so exciting to me. Finding food where I didn't know it existed: this is a gift that being vegetarian has given to me. I don't think I would have seen banana blossoms as edible before choosing to give up meat, because I was born an omnivore on Long

Island. Being a vegetarian food writer, though, and moving around the world, making friends wherever they may be, has made gastronomy and ecology open up to me like a banana blossom, revealing layers upon layers of beauty where I hadn't known to look for it.

There is so much diversity in the natural world that has been stamped out by agribusiness and its force-feeding of a meat-based Standard American Diet upon the population of the United States, a diet which like a disease has spread further around the world through neocolonialism and cultural imperialism. This is a book about claiming biodiversity and rebuilding the food system in a way that supports culture, tradition, and gastronomy. This is a book about what it means to remove meat from the center of our plates: If we do that, what do we find?

The United Nations' International Panel on Climate Change (IPCC) told us in August of 2021 that a warming of 1.5 degrees Celsius is inevitable—but that we have time to change industrial structures to prevent more warming.[1] In 2020, in a special report titled *Climate Change and Land*, the IPCC told us that the food system is a major cause of global warming—attributable for 21–37 percent of total greenhouse gas emissions—and that all of us, every human, should move toward a plant-based diet rather than a meat-based one.[2] It's been clear for over fifty years that the way land is used for farming—80 percent of farmed land is used to grow feed for livestock, which provides only 18 percent of the world's calories supply and 37 percent of its protein supply—is inefficient. This inefficient monoculture, as the cultivation of single crops is known, has dire consequences for our global ecosystem, global hunger and health, and the animals and insects whose robust existence is complementary to our human one.[3]

Because the inefficiency of this way of growing and consuming food has been known for so long, many people decided to change how they eat in order to get a head start on a rapidly encroaching future in which meat must return to its old status as a luxury good, in which dairy must come from different sources and not just cows, and in which eggs aren't laid by hens in tiny cages and male chicks aren't sent down chutes to die. A world in which animals aren't confined to factory farming operations and fed genetically modified corn, then processed by underpaid and overworked meat-processing workers, is a different world than what we in the United States have become accustomed to, of course. Luckily, these people who've gotten a head start on eating for a different future have laid the groundwork for thinking through what that world looks like—that world where we don't have a meat-based diet.

I don't care about meat. That should be said sooner rather than later. Eating meat is the default in Western cultures. What is compelling about making the default decision? Nothing, at least not to me. Jacques Derrida called the conditions for being understood as a full subject in the West "carno-phallogocentrism": being a meat-eater, being a man, and being an authoritative, speaking self. I'm only one of these, but I can be authoritative, and I can be loud.[4]

I'm concerned with the alternative choices, the abstentions and refusals. Sometimes the alternative choices are rooted in ethical or spiritual foundations. Other times, political. These political foundations could be anarchist or fascist or anything in between.

Basically, there is more diversity of thought in the refusal of meat than in meat-eating by default, both as a way of thinking and in the diet itself. The diversity of thought and of diet are complementary; they feed off each other, support each other—the good and the bad. The delicious and the disgusting.

I believe there is in the recent history of meat refusal a way forward in our rapidly warming world. But it's all complicated, a history populated by a range of characters, a range of ideologies. Here, in this book, I will attempt to make sense of them.

⁀〇

When disaster strikes, attention goes to life's essential forces—what grows and what flows—and the climate crisis is a disaster of the highest order. Food and drink are our most basic needs, and that never becomes more clear than when there is a crisis. After the devastation wrought by Hurricane Maria in Puerto Rico, an SOS written in chalked letters on concrete, large enough to be seen from a plane overhead, read, "Necesitamos Agua/Comida!!" (We Need Water/Food!!). *We need to survive*, this means.[5] Nothing more and nothing less.

Despite food being the means for survival, in day-to-day life, it's regarded rather flippantly. Food is considered feminine when outside the masculine environs of a restaurant kitchen. Cooking is a chore for many who spend all day laboring, and the idea of taking eating seriously is regarded as bourgeois affectation: something nice for people with money and time, but everyone else has to just stuff something in their mouths and get on with their lives. Being concerned with the provenance of one's food, too, is seen as classist, and discussing nutrition leads almost directly to fatphobia. Given the reality of food apartheid, which keeps mainly Black, brown, and Indigenous communities from having access to fresh fruits and vegetables, making overtures about going to the farmers' market is wildly out of touch with reality. I understand why many would prefer to keep their ears closed to the exploitation endemic to the global food system rather than concern themselves with the myriad ways in which we could be resisting and acting against its horrors. But the reality is that these horrors affect us all.

There is a lot to learn from crises and disasters that have already happened. When war broke out in Syria in 2011, the price of meat climbed 650 percent.[6] In its place, many cultivated mushrooms. Traditional Hawaiian foodways were nearly wiped out with the arrival of Europeans, and now they are using the Polynesian breadfruit to restore cultural traditions, the ecosystem, and local health.[7] During the war in the early 1990s, a Bosnian brewery became the sole source of water for many residents of Sarajevo.[8] A lifeline, where once there was only beer, which many see as a vice.

Examples of resilience in the face of large-scale catastrophe are necessarily small. The only way to have large-scale responses that serve local ecologies, economies, and traditions would be to radically transform the global economy away from fossil fuels and capitalism toward a much more collectively oriented political system that does not solely prioritize growth and profit but sees the value in culture and keeping the planet alive. Food could be at the heart of this transformation.

During the COVID-19 pandemic, which affected the citizens of nations rich and poor alike, we saw how significant food can be. President Donald Trump declared the meat-processing industry an essential business in the spring of 2020.[9] Mutual aid groups sprung up all over the United States and other countries to ensure communities had access to fresh food and hot meals. Community fridges emerged on streets. Nonetheless, food insecurity in the US hit record numbers.[10] Imagine if these types of efforts were supported by state infrastructure. Imagine if communities were empowered to create food justice in their areas through collective funding and organization.

In the meantime, as we work for the kinds of systemic changes that would ensure all of the food we eat is as good for the planet and workers as it is for us, there are ways to respond to the powerful lobbies that don't want to see agricultural or meat-processing workers paid a fair wage or ensure that farmland is used for a diversity of ingredients rather than just corn and soy. In the United States, the average person consumes 220 pounds of meat per year, and the meat and dairy industries receive subsidies from the government totaling $38 billion per year.[11] There is a rich history of resistance to industrial agriculture and its horrors, and if there is much more work to be done, this history shows us that change is possible.

For me, all stories about food are stories about appetite and nostal-gia—even when we're talking about global warming, and even when we're talking about the ways in which the state enables systemic oppression of humans, animals, and land. Talking about what we eat cannot just be rooted in the political; by its very nature, eating is per-sonal. This is why a delicate balance must be struck when we discuss ideas of ethical consumption in an unethical global food system that interacts with other systems of oppression, from white supremacy to patriarchy to capitalism. I have to start with myself, with my place in the world as a human being and a political subject, to make any sense. And my own eating life begins, as so many other eating lives do, with my maternal grandmother.

Grandma fed me lamb chops whenever I asked for them. We watched Julia Child and *The Frugal Gourmet* on PBS from bed. She thought it was funny how quickly a tiny three-year-old body could devour a whole lobster, its flesh dipped in hot melted butter, using her grubby baby hands. Like most, I was born an omnivore, trained to be open to all the food the world had to offer, whether it was the flesh of a baby animal or a crustacean that had to be boiled alive. And I wanted to take up that torch my grandmother gave me and eat the world. I wanted to be a gourmand. But then one day in my twenties, I looked upon a piece of meat and no longer saw food.

At that moment I saw flesh and stopped eating meat. I put down the torch and thought myself doomed to a life of tofu scrambles col-ored with turmeric to trick the eye into believing these were eggs, and gyros filled with stomach-bombing spiced seitan. Those were the foods I saw the vegetarians and vegans around me eating, and to me, they were poor imitations that misused centuries-old ingredients with origins in distinct cuisines. I had never been shown a way of not eating meat that foregrounded good ingredients and big flavor, despite the rich variety of vegetarian dishes in the cuisines of nations like India and China. To me, eating well had always been synonymous with eating anything and everything, from land and sea. Making this change in my life required not just new restrictions but finding a new way to create abundance.

There were a few false starts and more than a few bad meals, yet I found a new way to be that gourmand whose diet is based in plants, and this has become my life's purpose: showing people life without meat is still a beautiful life, a filling life, a satisfying life. One can find the bounty that is locally available and create magic. It's been more than a decade now of this decision that some call a lifestyle, others an ideology. I remember but do not long for the taste of meat. I can't imagine ever looking down at my plate again and seeing a piece a flesh. My consciousness has changed, and with it, my life. For me, not eating meat is part of my lifestyle, sure, as well as an ideology. Being a food writer who tackles this niche has also granted me an audience, a community. Not eating meat, though, is also so much more than this. The concerns I have, the concerns that keep me from throwing a steak into my cast-iron rather than tempeh, are manifold: ethical, spiritual, environmental, economic, political.

Vegetarianism and veganism, as practices, have roots in all those matters. To stop eating meat for ethical reasons means that one does not want to kill animals for their flesh. In the spiritual realm, giving up meat is often an aspect of living simply and cheaply; in cookbooks by religious people, whether Catholic or Buddhist, there are many easy recipes that encourage the eater to meditate on how the food made it to their plate. Environmental concerns are perhaps the most popular these days, as livestock production accounts for a good chunk of the food system's estimated 30 percent of anthropogenic, or human-caused, greenhouse gas emissions.[12] The political is a bit more complex, but for ecofeminists and anarchists, not eating meat has been a means of resisting and rejecting industrial agriculture, capitalism, and patriarchy.

My own rejection of meat finds roots in each of these concerns, and each will be rigorously explained and interrogated in this book. The intention of this book is to change how you think of meat, whether you eat it or do not. For those who wish to continue eating meat, I want to ask them to stop eating the industrially produced, factory-farmed kind. The amount of meat and the type of meat that is broadly consumed in the United States was created to fulfill the desires of capital, not our bodies, and we are coming to a crucial moment in the life of the planet. Change must happen, now.

Sometimes I think the only reason I have to be concerned with my choice to no longer eat meat is simply that most people have not made that choice, and often, I resent that it is considered a special choice in need of accommodation when, to me, it is the rational one. Of course, it wasn't easy to get to this point.

I tried as a teenager to give up meat, but it never stuck. My little brother would wave chicken wings in my face; my mom would make my favorite *pastelillos*, stuffed with *sazón*-seasoned ground beef and studded with olives. Then I would be done, back onto the Standard American Diet and ordering chicken fingers when I went to eat at the diner. To reject meat was to reject the nourishment I was being offered by those who loved me; it meant to separate myself from friends and family. Not eating what is served is understood as an affront. As Anthony Bourdain's famous "Grandma rule" goes, you eat what someone offers you. As a teenager without money (or, who refused to spend her money on anything other than CDs), my only choice was to eat what was served. In the United States, what is served rarely excludes a piece of meat. It would take years before my family would really take my veganism seriously, to understand it. By then, I was a vegetarian anyway, for which everyone breathed a sigh of relief.

These lapses in my meatlessness would turn me into a nihilist, convinced the vegetarian position was a pointless one, a futile pursuit of goodness in a bad world. When a breakfast would show up before me in a diner, slight horror would set upon my face as I realized there were three kinds of animal product on my plate: eggs, sausage, bacon. But then I ate it all, because this was the world I lived in, and I felt I had no choice but to go along with it. I have a vivid memory of arguing with a vegetarian friend (on her birthday, of all days) that one person's diet doesn't really make a difference if everyone else keeps picking up ground beef and chicken breasts at the supermarket. Taking that leap didn't make sense to me because it wouldn't fix the whole system. Now I know how to do the delicate dance, to show how individual choices work as tiny bricks thrown against the windows of tyranny. Still, quitting meat is a hard sell when it represents so much in the broad culture and eating meat is, admittedly, a hugely pleasurable act. There can still be pleasure, though—even this specific pleasure—in a way of eating that takes into account larger systems and the cumulative consequences of the industrial scale at which we've come to produce and process meat.

I've always been able to recognize the guilt in omnivores' comments to me because I was once one of them. There's logic to the strain of argument I had used with my vegetarian friend: What difference do our individual consumer choices really make? How can we go up against a massive industrial system of meat and dairy by ourselves, when they have high-powered lobbyists in legislators' ears? And, anyway, don't we need all the protein?

That's an argument people still make all the time. "Corporations alone are responsible for 71 percent of greenhouse gas emissions. It's not my responsibility to go vegetarian or vegan," is a common viral-tweet refrain. These have always been the standard retorts, and they are what I'll be arguing against in this book. My response now is to say that our lives, our ways of eating, will have to change if those corporations are held to account for those emissions—and we don't know when that might happen. We each have a personal role to play in making things a little easier on the planet.

The reason being vegetarian originally appealed to me was because it seemed like the cool thing to do. I wanted to be alternative; I wanted to be like the cool kids. With a friend named Merette, whom I idolized, I went to see Moby live at a small local venue before his album *Play* blew up, and there I got a glimpse of what I wanted. The drummer's shaved head was dyed in a leopard-spot pattern; an older female bass player had a "GIULIANI SUCKS" sticker on her guitar.

After the concert, I pored over the album's liner notes, in which Moby wrote about veganism. My teenage brain interpreted veganism as the ticket to belonging in that subculture.

It was also with my friend Merette, who had a car before she had a license, that I first went to a café in a town called Port Jefferson, located north of where we lived on Long Island. Our hometown of Patchogue offered nothing interesting to bored kids, making Port Jeff, as it was called, a go-to hang for local teenagers. The café was called Tiger Lily and was painted in swirls of lime green and bright orange paint, and there were pictures of Ani DiFranco everywhere. The women who worked there wore cut-up clothes and had hair dyed in all the wild colors of the late nineties, and though they served meat (it would be hard to survive on Long Island otherwise), it was the first place that I saw tofu outside of a Japanese restaurant. They put it in a wrap with crunchy carrot sticks, lettuce, and an orange-ginger dressing, and I ate mine with a fruity iced tea that felt like the height of sophistication at a time when usually I would have requested a Dr Pepper. I wanted to eat things like that, because to eat things like that would mean I was also cool, even if my Catholic school's dress code wouldn't let me dye my hair blue. Being vegetarian or vegan would give me something to have in common with the kids in bands I also thought were so ahead of their time, so rebellious, when all I did was play violin in the school orchestra. Nothing about my outer appearance suggested that I was cool. This decision would, I figured.

When I eventually gave up meat as an adult, I also gave up eggs and dairy, becoming a strict vegan of the kind Moby would outline in his liner notes. Veganism at that time appealed to me because it was in line with the ethics I was adopting as an obsessive practitioner of Ashtanga yoga. *May all beings everywhere be happy and free*, we said at the end of each class. The hypocrisy of saying that, of believing in my desire for it to be true and still eating flesh, was too much to bear. I gave up all animal products, started a vegan bakery, and became, eventually, a writer on plant-based food. This meant that there was pressure on me to be a perfect vegan, something I couldn't keep up when life and learning got in the way.

The first time I willingly ate an oyster after five years of strict veganism, I walked out onto a Midtown Manhattan street and envisioned a clock inside my body winding backward. All the effort of those years, all the times I followed my convictions in refusing food that family and friends offered me suddenly seemed meaningless. There was guilt, shame, and fear in me—the sense that I'd undone not just years of dedication to veganism as an ethic but also undone myself. This way of eating and living had become an inextricable part of my identity: when I wasn't a good person in other ways, when I wasn't the greatest friend or sister or partner, I still could point to this constant effort I expended toward being kind to animals, to the planet, to my ongoing boycott of industrial animal agriculture and its labor abuses. Now, I had none of that.

What drove me to eat the oyster was personal grief after the death of my younger brother. What I felt after eating it was political failure. My response was utterly dramatic—oysters are pretty sustainably farmed, and some people even consider them vegan—but it was in line with how important this decision I'd made was to me. I'd committed to it over and over again, even when it was alienating. It was this intense emotional response, though, that would show me a different way to live out my ethics.

Since that time, I have come to understand eating with the planet and animals in mind as a practice rather than a strict set of rules that must be followed to the letter at all times, no matter one's circumstances or geography. Eating ethically is an effort, a constant attempt to make choices regarding the consumption of food and goods that treads as lightly on the planet as possible while doing the least harm to humans and nonhuman animals. That means, of course, the most obvious thing: avoiding animal products. But it also means concern for the labor rights of farmworkers and the land rights of Indigenous and Black people, as well as a recognition of the necessity of access to fresh, local, culturally appropriate food and clean water for all the world's people. Not eating meat is to seek balance in ecology and the relationships between humans and nonhuman animals. That's why moments in which our resolve breaks down, whether because we're tired or broke or in mourning, can feel so shameful. That's also why omnivores will make any possible argument to delegitimize the practice: they see it as a pursuit of purity, of perfection. I reject this absolutist framework. Vegetarianism and veganism are mutable, adaptable.

These days, I am a vegetarian, happy to eat eggs from locally raised chickens or goat cheese from a local farmer to support the food economy in Puerto Rico, where 85 percent of what's available has been imported from the United States or Europe via the United States, making a long and dispiriting trek to supermarkets. As I will outline in the book, supporting local food economies and the pursuit of food sovereignty for historically and consistently colonized lands (such as Puerto Rico) should be a part of practicing meatless eating. To be plant-based should not just mean rejecting industrial agriculture; it should encompass supporting local agriculture that allows for biodiversity and dignified lives for farmers.

Many new companies have adopted the phrase "plant-based" to get away from the connotations of "vegan" or "vegetarian," which have long been the subject of pop culture jokes and derision. "How will you know if someone is vegan?" begins a common one. "Don't worry, they'll tell you." Never mind that anecdotally, I and others who don't eat meat can tell you that nothing will make a person talk more about their love for beef than the simple statement at a dinner party, "Thank you, but I don't eat meat," as a slice of steak is offered.

But the whole plant-based-product thing is focused solely on consumption, on buying the right oat milk or soy burger that bleeds at fast-food restaurants as a means of "saving the planet" while lining the pockets of the corporations that manufacture those goods. In an era of food-system confusion, the phrase "plant-based" has emerged as a cure, but its meaning can be obscured by greenwashing. What it means, exactly, is up to the eater: while in some cases, this means a fully vegan diet that completely excludes animal products, in others, it means, simply, a diet mainly of plants. This approach could also be called "flexitarianism" and also applies to Mark Bittman's suggestion to be "vegan before 6:00." It means "vegan without veganism"—a style of consumption without the baggage of its cultural connotations.

Plant-based companies prioritize purchasing power and leave behind the sense of "weirdness" that has glommed onto meatless eating since it emerged into popular consciousness in the United States. Think of how much not eating meat is associated with being a "hippie" or living on a commune: these are ideas that US society at large doesn't like because it values what we can achieve collectively rather than individually. That weirdness has endured precisely because vegetarianism and veganism reject the consumerist, efficiency-driven, labor-abusing, environmentally taxing status quo upon which the US food system is based—a status quo supported through government subsidies and advertising, as well as more insidious cultural ties to patriarchy, white supremacy, and imperialism. If to be "weird" means to not participate in the pillage of the earth's natural resources, then yes: not eating meat and focusing on local agriculture rather than industrialized food is weird.

Nothing that can be bought will prove a solution to the greenhouse gas emissions caused by a centralized, globalized food system that prioritizes efficiency yet still leaves 854 million people on the planet undernourished and twenty-five thousand people per day dying of hunger.[13] That is why the idea of the "plant-based diet"—whether vegan, vegetarian, or flexible—needs to be reinvigorated and understood as a political stance that rejects efficient but profit-driven industrialized agriculture as much as it abhors the slaughter of confined animals.

When I started to write about food and research the reasons people eat meat in the first place, I realized that the same impulse toward cultural belonging that I sought out by rejecting meat was the reason most people loved to have a steak on their plate. Eating a veggie burger meant I was radical; eating a beef burger meant being mainstream. Flavor was and is secondary to symbolism when it comes to eating meat or rejecting it. Though the consumption of animals is historically tied up with human evolution—indeed, it was what allowed us to become human—according to Josh Berson, author of *The Meat Question: Animals, Humans, and the Deep History of Food*, it's been an economic imperative more than a natural one.[14]

Meat represents wealth, virility, masculinity, conquer, empire. The richer a nation becomes, the more meat the population consumes, and that's why right now we are at a crucial point at which meat consumption must decrease or the planet's warming will not cease, and the human race will be left fighting for scarce resources in an uninhabitable climate. There is nothing natural about eating animal products for breakfast, lunch, and dinner. I'll never forget hearing the chef Carla Hall introduce her cookbook *Carla Hall's Soul Food: Everyday and Celebration* at the Brownsville Community Culinary Center in Brooklyn and tell the audience that a family who kept chickens half a century ago wouldn't have eaten chicken every night. The animals were too valuable for that because of the eggs they provided. This was a radical statement from a chef who came to fame on TV, through *Top Chef* and *The Chew*. It made me realize there was a shift happening, though it was coming small and slow. Eventually, I thought, it won't be so strange to hear these words from a chef.

As the Beat poet Diane di Prima wrote in "Rant," "the war against the imagination" is what's most significant—a cultural battle. Once people think of meatless food as food, as worthy of their attention and their meals, imagine how much the world will change. A diet based on plants is a diet of diversity, of abundance and opportunity, of innovation. There are so many varieties of beans, of rice, of grains. In my years of writing about vegan cuisine, I've been to a grocery store in the Bronx staffed by practicing Rastafarians; an ecofeminist restaurant in Connecticut; a taco shop in Mexico City that makes chorizo out of mushrooms; fine-dining "plant-based" and punk mushroom spots in Buenos Aires; and a local vegetarian café among tire shops in San Juan. I've eaten the "vegetable-forward" cooking of master male chefs, studied the vegetarian cookbooks of women, and eaten tagliatelle made from chickpea flour in the hills of Tuscany. Everywhere I've gone, I've found the vegetables, and in finding them, I've found new flavor, new techniques, and new philosophies. To eat plants is to be open to the world. It is, to me, to be the same child my grandma taught me to be, just with a different item in the center of my plate—and, contrary to jokes omnivores might make, it's not always a bland slab of tofu.

There is more to be done on political and economic grounds, of course: governments must regulate carbon emissions and fossil fuel use. Individual consumption isn't causing the climate crisis; it's the conditions of individual consumption that are causing it. But if these conditions are changed by states that act upon our dire situation, there will be, by necessity, less meat and dairy available for the eating. Diets will change, whether we like it or not. I believe there's meaning in changing before it gets that bad, whether you look at your steak and see deliciousness or, like me, see a dead cow.

Because of the climate crisis (and the COVID-19 pandemic) and because people are slow to change their behaviors without being forced to, entire new industries have cropped up to make sure no one misses a chicken nugget. There are tech burgers like those made by Impossible Foods and Beyond Meat, which are now widely accessible in fast food and finer dining alike, as well as cultured meat, which is made in a lab using the cells of animals themselves. The companies getting into the business of making "planet-friendly" plant-based meat eschew the labels of "vegan" or "vegetarian" and base their products on single ingredients like genetically modified soy or pea protein, thus encouraging questionable farming practices that we know deplete soil health. They also don't use their ethical clout to encourage changes to broader fast-food practices, like setting fair worker wages or sourcing better-quality versions of the animal products they continue to sell. These companies are making money, but is anything really changing?

Yes, things are changing. Because these products, though a stopgap on the way to eating a truly diverse plant-based diet, represent a broad cultural recognition that we need to decrease our meat consumption. Those omnivores I know who will turn their nose up at fake meat are still thrilled to eat a dinner where the veggie burgers are recognizably composed of vegetables and grains; they will happily make a seared steak of eggplant their main course. The world, the people, are changing, but I want more. I think more is possible.

This book is about putting meatless diets in the US in their cultural and culinary context. We're not just talking about hippies who would put carob in a cookie rather than chocolate chips, or the folks at The Farm commune in Tennessee who made cheese from nutritional yeast and tofu—though they do appear in the book. But there are also the ecofeminists of the second wave who gave up meat when they divorced their husbands. There are the anarchist punks of the 1980s, who wanted to smash the state with recipes for massive pots of three-bean chili that they would serve to the bands crashing on their living room floors. We're also talking about the chefs from the aughts through now who have turned veganism from a punchline into a cuisine all its own, where the ingredients are as farm-to-table as any omnivorous chefs', and the techniques used just as complex.

But when you talk about the good, you also need to talk about the bad. The "wellness" movement and diet culture have co-opted plant-based cooking to make it into something restrictive, something fatphobic, rather than a way to live in abundance. There are ecofascists and neo-Nazis who espouse veganism as a means of maintaining racial "purity." There are conservative vegans who won't eat meat but will be in favor of the death penalty, as though a human could ever deserve to be killed. And there are those companies that—though well-intentioned—want to mold veganism and vegetarianism into capitalism's image rather than use it to end oppression in all forms.

Not eating meat has been, for more than fifty years now, deeply associated with the counterculture in the United States—and now it's going in a mainstream direction. How can it retain its place as a radical rejection of industrial agriculture, as a way of living that is connected to the earth, the animals, our fellow humans? In short, how can it support agroecology? I believe it has to, if we're going to reverse the effects of climate change and enter into a new relationship with eating and with the earth. Meatless eating can stay weird, I say, even as it becomes more and more commodified.

1. DIET FOR WHOSE PLANET?

Frances Moore Lappé didn't necessarily intend to define how we discuss the effects of food consumption on the environment, but that is precisely what she did with the 1971 publication of the first edition of *Diet for a Small Planet*, which has sold more than three million copies and been translated into half a dozen languages. In 2021, its fiftieth anniversary edition was released (it included my contribution of a recipe for vegan salted chocolate almond cookies), proving its ongoing significance to the cultural dialogue around the ethics of eating. How did that happen, and what is this text's real legacy?

What started as a one-page handout in the 1960s became an influential text for popularizing the idea that meat was a "protein factory in reverse," amounting to significant inefficiencies in how calories are provided to eaters. The grain used to feed the livestock that became meat, she wrote, could be used to feed people. (More accurately, the land used to grow grain for livestock could be used to grow a diverse array of plant food for people.) In stating this plainly, Lappé transformed the food conversation.

Meatless eating in the United States didn't begin with *Diet for a Small Planet*, but the book marked a turning point with a well-argued, new explanation for why people should eschew animal products most of the time. She made it global, and she made it about hunger, and what she said resonated deep and wide among the middle class. "Most people think of vegetarianism as an ethical stance against the killing of animals, unconventional, and certainly untraditional," Lappé wrote.[1] "But what I advocate is the return to the traditional diet on which our bodies evolved. Traditionally the human diet has centered on plant foods, with animal foods playing a supplementary role." That's something a lot of folks could get behind, because it didn't turn them into the well-trodden stereotype of a "humorless" vegetarian (which would eventually give birth to the "fanatical vegan"). Lappé made sensible the idea of eating with ecology in mind, showing that a choice to center meatless meals in one's life could yield results rich in both flavor and impact.

The book's central argument wasn't whether or not eating animals is morally acceptable; Lappé herself didn't (and still doesn't) identify as a vegetarian: what was important, really, was whether everyone on the planet had access to sufficient food. The best way to do that would be with minimal animal protein and otherwise "complementary proteins" derived from plant sources. She wanted people and organizations to do away with "simplistic overpopulation theories of hunger," and in that, she was successful (though ecofascism, which we will get to later, still has a foothold in the vegan movement). Now, "overpopulation" as a cause for not just hunger but climate change is seen as a myth driven by white supremacy that allows the rich nations of the Global North a scapegoat for its own overconsumption and hoarding of resources.

The nutritional science regarding the notion of complementary proteins did prove to be off. This theory asserts that no plant protein is "complete"—meaning it contains the nine amino acids our bodies can't produce on its own—and so, to get those amino acids we have to eat, for example, brown rice with lentils. Debunking this really entrenched idea that protein from plants is somehow inferior has been an ongoing struggle for nutritionists and anyone who tries to tell people to eat less meat. Our bodies actually, regardless of what we eat, can create all the amino acids we need to have a functional amount of protein, so long as we're eating sufficient "whole" foods—vegetables, fruits, grains, legumes. Lappé corrected herself in the tenth-anniversary 1981 edition, but considering the success of the first edition, this mistake has remained part of the conversation on whether a vegan or vegetarian diet can provide enough protein. When I first went vegan in 2011, I was obsessed with making sure I had a "complete" protein every day—whether it was quinoa or some combination of grain and legume—because that's what all the literature I was reading continued to tell me. Over time, by doing more reading and falling into less restrictive eating habits, I realized that wasn't necessary.

The question of whether to eat "complementary" protein ended up beside the point anyway. The book created a novel way of considering global and personal food systems. Throughout the '70s, the *New York Times* in particular ran many stories about families deciding to give vegetarianism a try, citing her book. In 1974, a piece by Maya Pines ran under the headline "Meatless, Guiltless: A Family Pursues Economics, Health, and Compassion by Joining the New Vegetarians." The article showed Lappé's influence explicitly, and it gave a name to what she created: the new vegetarians, as opposed to the old. It marked a fresh start for the vegetarian movement in the United States.

As Jonathan Kauffman writes in *Hippie Food: How Back-to-the-Landers, Longhairs, and Revolutionaries Changed the Way We Eat*, "Vegetarians since [nineteenth-century vegetarian advocate] Sylvester Graham's day had put forward scores of arguments that a vegetarian diet would produce vigorous, athletic, fertile bodies, but no one had before made the case with figures that scientific research could confirm. More broadly than that, few nutrition writers up until that point had written about food in such overtly political terms."[2] It was the combination of science, nutrition, and agricultural knowledge that made Lappé so influential in a specific milieu.

As the decade wore on, more and more vegetarian cookbooks were released, natural food stores proliferated across the country, and this way of eating with all of humanity in mind stopped seeming like a fool's errand. As I've read her book after years of practicing veganism or vegetarianism and reading about our food system, I realize that her perspective has seeped into everyone else I've read or listened to: in writing this book, she created a new blueprint for talking about our personal and political roles in the global food system.

But it was quite definitively a blueprint for a particular time and audience—white middle-class people living in the US who had been raised to believe that meat was the most functional way to consume sufficient protein, and for whom eating meat meant status and satiety: comfort, in sum. For many in this demographic before and after *Diet for a Small Planet*, a "decent meal"—one that meets both nutritional and cultural needs—has included meat. That hadn't been the case for many people throughout history, though.

The earliest recorded vegetarians lived in ancient India and practiced the Hindu and Jain religions. There is also evidence that it was somewhat prevalent in ancient Greece, practiced by a group known as the Pythagoreans, after the creator of the famous mathematical theorem we're taught in algebra class. Eschewing meat fell out of favor in Europe, except among monks, but eventually made a resurgence in the nineteenth century, when the first vegetarian society was formed in Britain.

It was in the nineteenth century, too, that vegetarianism emerged in the US through British members of the Bible Christian Church who had emigrated in search of more religious freedom. Just as vegetarian eating had been presented as an ethical choice before Lappé, it had also usually been a matter of spiritual purity, as in the cases of Sylvester Graham or John Harvey Kellogg, a Presbyterian and a Seventh-Day Adventist, respectively.

According to *The Vegetarian Crusade: The Rise of an American Reform Movement, 1817–1921*, by Adam D. Shprintzen, this move set off the beginnings of vegetarianism in the newly formed republic.[3] "The activities of this small band of dissidents would lead to the development of a much larger movement in the United States, focusing on one particular component of the church's doctrine, the abstention from meat," Shprintzen writes. "Proto-vegetarianism—the individuals and groups who would lay the foundations of a vegetarian movement in the United States—began with the arrival of the Bible Christians." The Graham and Kellogg types.

Through speeches, publications, and public meetings, people preaching proto-vegetarianism worked "to illustrate the larger social and political implications of dietary choices." While this was mainly a religious pursuit, as vegetarianism had been through history connected to religion or philosophical cults, there is no doubt this was the setup for the future of a politically minded and secular vegetarianism. And when one looks at the twentieth century, it was Lappé who ushered in that nonreligious moment for giving up meat.

While it was a watershed moment, the media's focus on Lappé's groundbreaking work tends to overlook an activist movement toward eating for the planet that was already taking shape. *Diet for a Small Planet* provided a cohesive, accessible argument against the industrialized, centralized ways in which agriculture had scaled up, creating a situation in which more grain was fed to livestock than to humans, but that was a problem created by the very people to whom Lappé was speaking: those whose affluence was built upon the convenience conjured by big farms and supermarkets. This was a creation of the Global North, and of the United States in particular. It was by prioritizing a meat-first diet that this situation came into play. Black communities, Indigenous peoples, and other people of color have been aware of this displacement of traditional foodways and have historically used their diets as a form of resistance, despite how much a focus on local, seasonal ingredients and vegetable-forward cooking has been discounted.

As chef, food-justice activist, and cookbook author Bryant Terry told me in an interview for my podcast, "When you hear about these types of dietary practices and political positions, I think a lot of people default towards people like Peter Singer and John Robbins and

Frances Moore Lappé, and, you know, they certainly are important thinkers and activists and have inspired a lot of my work—two of them being personal mentors. But I just always have to pivot back to: my early teachers were all Black folks."[4]

The 1960s were a time of deep and extensive conversation about the role of food and diet in forming a Black national identity. Elijah Muhammad, leader of the Nation of Islam, put out *How to Eat to Live, Book No. 1* in 1967, and advocated for moving away from "soul food" and any food associated with slavery, most prominently pork, and gradually came to advocate for a vegetarian diet as the most healthful. Muhammad and Malcolm X both used meat consumption as a means of differentiating Black people from whites, specifically the brutal means of slaughter without any ritual or compassion that had come into practice with industrial animal agriculture. "When I was a little boy, I lived on a farm with white folks. When they shoot something, they just go crazy, you know, like they were really getting their kicks," Malcolm X said in a 1964 speech.[5]

This trend toward vegetarianism among Black people continued in the '70s, with no mention of Lappé as an influencing force in the *Ebony* article "A Farewell to Chitterlings: Vegetarianism Is on the Rise Among Diet-Conscious Blacks."[6] Althea Smith's piece focused on the slimming and energy effects of a meatless diet for her subjects, which included Dick Gregory, whose 1974 book *Natural Diet for Folks Who Eat: Cookin' with Mother Nature* was widely read and continues to be referenced as one of the most significant texts of Black vegetarianism from its time. He was inspired by the naturopath Alvenia M. Fulton to believe in diet as part of civil rights activism, "believing that bad diets bolstered the forces of white supremacy by weakening or killing black bodies," as Jennifer Jensen Wallach wrote in her 2014 piece, "How to Eat to Live: Black Nationalism and the Post-1964 Culinary Turn."[7]

As vegetarianism was hitting the mainstream in the '70s because of a confluence of cultural and political forces from numerous sides (disaffection with the Vietnam War and its impacts on young people cannot be discounted), what was known as "countercultural cuisine" was developing in Black communities separately from white ones:

> Black nationalist and white countercultural eaters used food prac-
> tices as a way to demonstrate their disaffection with American
> culture, but they generally differed in their prescriptions for better
> alternatives. Proponents of what [historian Warren] Belasco labels
> "countercuisine" developed a set of unconventional food practices
> as a way to establish identities on the margins of mainstream cul-
> ture and to reject domination by a centralized power structure.
> White counterculture eaters did not propose an alternative national
> identity. In contrast, black nationalist eaters saw their food practices
> as an aspect of nation-building. They wanted to create a black na-
> tion that operated in lockstep, unified by ideological and cultural
> goals. Black culinary radicals used ideas about food as a means to
> opt out of white U.S. culture and into a black cultural nation.[8]

That these movements were happening in tandem shows how incorrect entrenched narratives about the whiteness of veganism and vegetarianism are. Terry is right that the names people bring up, Lappé included, are all white. But this is shifting to more accurately reflect the history of meatless eating: in January 2021, Amirah Mercer wrote for *Eater* about finding empowerment in the Black history of plant-based diets: "Within the last 20 years, knowledge of plant-based eating has seeped into Black American life like a finely steeped herbal tea. Black-owned vegan restaurants have been flourishing across the country, in the process dissolving some of the barriers to entry to a way of life that could radically shift how Black Americans take care of themselves."[9]

Why, though, has *Diet for a Small Planet* been updated and re-released for its fifth, tenth, twentieth, and now fiftieth anniversary editions instead of *Dick Gregory's Natural Diet for Folks Who Eat*? Why has the concept of "white veganism" had such a strong cultural hold? The European colonizers were the ones who created the style of farming that has led to an inefficient meat-based diet, yet white people have led the charge for a plant-based diet in the US despite the historical reality that this way of eating has deep roots in Africa, Asia, and Latin America. *Natural Diet for Folks Who Eat* was reissued in 2021, so there is finally a narrative shift occurring—a recognition more broadly of how significant a text it has been, that there has always been more diversity to the counterculture food story, once it's expanded to include the struggle for civil rights.

When one really gets into the history, it is clear that much more diversity lies behind the idea of eating in a way that doesn't harm animals. For my first restaurant review in the *Village Voice*, I decided to take the 5 train from Brooklyn all the way up to the Bronx to try out Vegan's Delight, which has now been open for nearly three decades. Nestled among various fast-food and pharmacy-chain establishments, it's known as a Rastafarian grocer that sells food that fits into the "Ital" diet established in Jamaica, which is a mainly vegetarian but often vegan diet, save maybe for some fresh-caught fish—and operates like a bodega, with a food counter and a market section. The menu featured dal patties, which had sold out by my 3 p.m. visit. Behind the counter, other options presented themselves: two shelves of thin orange pockets of flaky, curry-powder-spiked dough filled with spiced blends of tofu, ackee (a buttery fruit with a texture akin to jackfruit), vegetables, and soy-based "chicken," "beef," and "fish." I opted for the veggie patty, which is stuffed with cabbage and carrot, and sold for just three dollars.

Faux shrimp made of soy could be found in the grocery section. That form of fake shrimp was made possible by Buddhist innovation in the realm of meatless meat that began in China centuries ago. May Wah Vegetarian Market, now Lily's Vegan Pantry, founded in New York City in 1994, sells a ton of vegan seafood and other products, and—as food writer Clarissa Wei has reported for *Goldthread*—began because the founder, Lee Mee Ng, "struggled to find the kind of fake meat she grew up eating in Taiwan as a practicing Buddhist."[10]

If, in New York City, it's easy to trace vegan food from Chinatown to a Jamaican neighborhood in the Bronx, why is the image of veganism in most omnivores' heads so white? The answer could be as simple as, "because then it's easy to dismiss," and this would go along with the historical understanding of vegetarianism as synonymous with "crankiness," as Tristram Stuart wrote in his *The Bloodless Revolution*.[11] To Stuart, that's what made it easy to pigeonhole and ignore. Not much has changed in centuries. Not eating meat means, to many, being no fun. But never has it meant being white—not until recently.

Lisa Betty, a PhD candidate at Fordham University, published a scathing piece titled "Veganism* Is in Crisis" in February 2021, calling out white vegans whose approach isn't intersectional—meaning, aware of race, gender, colonialism, and other forms of systemic oppression—and narratives that erase communities of color who have historically or even contemporarily gone meatless. She wrote:

> Although scholar-activist works from Aph Ko, Syl Ko, A. Breeze Harper, and Omowale Adewale have organized, theorized and contextualized an expansive future of veganism as radical, shifting, just, and transformative—their work seems to be positioned as novelties in vegan movement spaces. Additionally, recently Decolonial Veganism, Intersectional Veganism and Radical Veganism has entered the visual mainstream through social media, which has been met with confusion from mostly white "nonhuman animal ONLY" vegans.[12]

The key point for me in Betty's piece that has big repercussions for how the success of *Diet for a Small Planet* has been enshrined is that the work of Black and brown vegans and vegetarians has been "positioned as novelties." This has occurred for the gastronomical writing of Black nationalists as well. Lappé's success came from creating a neutral argument, divorced from historical spiritual arguments and dominant ethical concerns about meat consumption. "Neutral" in the US means "white," though, and thus her success and push in the media overtook the conversation, setting up whiteness's continued dominance in vegetarian and vegan narratives. "Countercuisine" became a white thing, with places like Vegan's Delight and books like Gregory's and all those who came after regarded as "other" in an already "alternative" space.

There is more space now in the vegetarian and vegan narrative, because it's being carved out. Amy Quichiz of Veggie Mijas, a national women of color vegan collective, has garnered attention for helping Black, Latinx, and other people of color support each other in giving up meat, and her work began from understanding what she eats as part of bigger social justice movements.

"We can't live in a world where we're fighting for social justice while viewing animals as less than others," she told me for my podcast *Meatless* in 2019.[13] Her parents are from Colombia and Peru, and when she brought quinoa home to Jackson Heights, Queens, her father laughed, telling her that's what he ate when he was poor.

"I feel . . . that decolonizing your lifestyle is literally just going back to your roots, asking a lot of questions and asking where your food came from as well," she said. Quinoa was an ancestral food for her that white vegans had adopted, leading to it being sold at a premium price while also causing shortages for growers in Peru and Bolivia who were dependent on this grain for sustenance.

"Can vegans stomach the unpalatable truth about quinoa?" *The Guardian* asked in 2013.[14] At that time, the price had tripled, making imported food in those countries more affordable and leading to monocropping of historically diverse land. But the question should have specified *which* vegans had made a mess of the quinoa market. For Quichiz, eating quinoa meant decolonizing her own diet and going back to her roots, and she couldn't let these new "health food" connotations stop that.

"At the end of the day, if we're going back to our roots yet you're having that kind of concept, like, how much did white people take from you?" she said. "At the end of the day, how much did white people brainwash you to tell you that it's expensive and you can't have it? You, out of all people, can't have it?"

Dominant and "alternative" ways of eating in the US have thus had big effects abroad, on the very people historically colonized by Europe. It's an ongoing overreach, as the mindset in the US is that there will be some sort of miracle "superfood" that can be eaten in bulk but have no poor health or ecological effects. It's a consumer ideology that is ultimately always destructive. Americans, whether eating meat or not, should be influenced by the traditional diets of the rest of the world—but do so using local ingredients rather than over-importing staple grains from abroad.

Instead, the US has exported its agricultural practices, and many countries around the world have experienced a "nutrition transition," wherein a traditionally plant-based and localized diet moves toward one high in meat.[15] According to the Harvard School of Public Health, this phenomenon results from modernization, urbanization, economic development, and increased wealth—but ultimately leads to poor health outcomes as well as more homogeneous land use.

For example, Senegal, Chad, Mali, Sierra Leone, and other West African countries have cuisines so high in vegetables, fruits, grains, and legumes that a 2015 study published in *The Lancet* had those nations high on the list of the world's healthiest diets.[16] According to the UN Food and Agriculture Organization, meat consumption in Africa is projected to grow 30 percent by 2030.[17] As economies have allowed for a larger middle class in many African countries, though, more people have moved away from traditional diets and toward a Western-style diet high in meat.

This dietary transition has garnered a strong response across the continent from vegans and vegetarians who want to show off the beauty, ease, and better health that comes from traditional diets. Bloggers like Tomi Makanjuola, founder of *The Vegan Nigerian*; Afia Amoako, the author of the blog *The Canadian African*; and Tendai Chipara, the Zimbabwean author of *Plant-Based African*, all share recipes and stories, removing the small amount of meat that would traditionally be in dishes.

It is not just in Africa that a largely plant-based diet in line with ecological and farming needs has been traditional. In their introduction to the 2015 cookbook *Decolonize Your Diet: Plant-Based Mexican-American Recipes for Health and Healing*, authors Luz Calvo and Catriona Rueda Esquibel write that their way of eating is a response to and a way of working with the five hundred years of colonization of the Americas. "Throughout the Americas, colonization meant the transfer of land from Native peoples to Europeans, the death of millions of Indigenous people, rape of Native women, and the violent suppression of Indigenous knowledge, cultures," they write. "We recognize the importance of Indigenous knowledge and ways of being in the world and believe in the need to dismantle colonial systems of knowledge."[18]

Through the book, their approach to cooking—which, while vegetarian, doesn't exclude omnivores or pescatarians—is focused on getting away from processed foods created through industrial agriculture and recognizing the inherent plant-forward nature of Mexican American cuisine. The text is a reclamation, as well as a statement on the fact that white people in the US don't own vegetarian cooking, despite the narratives that have been sold over the last few decades.

The Indigenous scholar Margaret Robinson has written about the problem of constructing the ur-vegan as white when Indigenous foodways have been displaced by settler colonialism. In the chapter "Veganism and Mi'kmaq Legends" in *Meatsplaining: The Animal Agriculture Industry and the Rhetoric of Denial*, she quotes a few white men who "by projecting white imperialism onto vegans . . . enable white omnivores . . . to bond with Aboriginal people over meat-eating."[19] She continues:

> When veganism is constructed as white, Aboriginal people who eschew the use of animal products are depicted as sacrificing our cultural authenticity. This presents a challenge for those of us who

view our veganism as ethically, spiritually, and culturally compatible with our indigeneity. A second barrier to Aboriginal veganism is the portrayal of veganism as a product of class privilege. Opponents claim that a vegan diet is an indulgence since the poor (among whom Aboriginal people are disproportionately represented) must eat whatever is available and cannot afford to be so picky. This argument assumes that highly processed specialty products make up the bulk of a vegan diet. Such an argument also overlooks the economic and environmental cost of meat, and assumes that the subsidized meat and dairy industries in North America are representative of the world.

Robinson's concise description here mirrors the experiences of vegan bloggers in Africa, Quichiz's father's memories of quinoa, and the *Decolonize Your Diet*'s authors' realization that their ancestral foodways work with the earth, not against it, and make for healthy lives. But fighting against the creep of increased meat-eating that comes with affluence has proven a challenge, even in Asia, a historical home of plant-based meats.

In the 1960s, the average Chinese person ate less than 5 kilograms of meat per year, but consumption rose to 20 kilograms per capita by the late 1980s. Now, according to *Time* magazine, China consumes 28 percent of the world's meat—and half of all pork. That is a rapid nutrition transition, especially for a country with such a rich history of mock meat and using soy for protein. This increase in meat consumption has occurred as a result of the country opening up more to the West as well as higher incomes, and it's a telling trend across Asia, making it a big potential market for "tech" and lab meat.

By digging into the archives of SoyInfo Center, which has the most comprehensive database on and history of non-meat and non-dairy foods, one finds the history of soy and soy products on all continents by region. It has been put together by William Shurtleff and Akiko Aoyagi—who published *The Book of Tofu*, *The Book of Miso*, and *The Book of Tempeh* in the '70s (more on those later)—and is part of that wave of interest in more complex vegetarian eating. They have broken down how to make these ingredients from scratch, chronicled their histories, and included culturally appropriate recipes. Their work extends into the center's "bibliographies" of soy-based and other vegan foods.

According to their research, the use of soy in China and Taiwan dates back to 1024 BCE. Soy is the most significant signifier of non-meat foods because it was the first and continues to be the most popular. While soy milk has gone out of fashion in favor of almond and oat milk, tofu, yuba, and soy-based tempeh continue to be found at pretty much any vegetarian or vegan restaurant in the world. And it began in China, where vegetarian Buddhist monks would entertain omnivorous visitors with mock meats made from tofu or wheat gluten, commonly known as seitan. In Indonesia, tempeh, another staple meatless protein, was created from fermenting soybeans in banana leaves. Generally, giving up meat altogether has been considered an act of asceticism or a necessity of poverty, but using it sparingly as a way to add flavor and fat to a dish had been a major piece of the region's cultural gastronomy.

It's the flattening—perhaps monocropping, one could say—of the world into one diet, the dominant US diet that is so meat-heavy, that will be the challenge to overcome as the global food system changes by necessity. But creating one sole vegetarian and vegan narrative makes it so hard to deepen the cultural conversation around how to eat ethically, in a way that treads lightly on the planet and doesn't take away anyone's cultural traditions. The US doesn't represent the world, but its style of agricultural and gastronomic practices has sought to dominate a world originally rife with bio and culinary diversity.

It's deeply meaningful that there are more books and more conversation about how a plant-based rather than meat-based diet has been more commonplace in history and throughout a diverse array of cultures. Now we can understand that the increase in meat consumption that's occurred in the West over the last century has been constructed for the economic benefit of a few. Just as De Beers created the diamond engagement ring to sell jewels, we've been sold an endless supply of hamburgers to line the pockets of those in the beef and fast-food businesses. If we are to move forward toward a plant-based planet, which is a necessity, it needs to be a global coalition rededicated to biodiversity and a diet that reflects locality.

The UN Intergovernmental Panel on Climate Change (IPCC) made this known in its report *Climate Change and Land*. The panel wrote, "Healthy and sustainable diets are high in coarse grains, pulses, fruits and vegetables, and nuts and seeds; low in energy-intensive animal-sourced and discretionary foods (such as sugary beverages)."[20] The grains, pulses, fruits, and vegetables are less depleting to soil and yield more energy per calorie than animal-sourced foods. The study's authors also noted that the changes in diet are going to be dependent upon "consumer choices and dietary preferences that are guided by social, cultural, environmental, and traditional factors, as well as income growth." Basically: We have to get the plant foods in front of people, make them affordable, and radically alter the cultural status of meat in the West.

Lappé knew that this moment was coming when she published the first edition of *Diet for a Small Planet* back in 1971 and altered the cultural status of meat for some. But the number of people in the US who identify as vegetarian or vegan is still a tiny number: 5 to 8 percent identify as vegetarian, and 3 percent as vegan. (I take this statistic with a big grain of flaky sea salt, though, as no one's ever polled me.) People are willing to eat more meatless meals, though. Does that make a difference?

"About 21–37% of total greenhouse gas (GHG) emissions are attributable to the food system," the IPCC also wrote.[21] That includes all aspects of the food system, from the methods of agriculture from planting to processing to packaging and transport. Some pieces of that statistic make more of an impact than other pieces; beef, for example, accounts for 13 percent of livestock emissions. One aspect that has been downplayed, especially in the US media, is the transport.

Most studies put transport at only 10 percent of total emissions of the foods consumed in US households, which leads folks like *Washington Post* columnist Tamar Haspel to declare, "LOCAL FOODS AREN'T BETTER FOR THE CLIMATE!"[22] Pieces in online news and opinion outlets *Vox* and *Noema* echo this sentiment against localism, focusing solely on an efficiency in long-distance food transport that discounts a lot of significant effects of becoming engaged in local agriculture and its potential resilience during catastrophe.[23] Yes, the emissions are mainly happening in production. The most important thing is what you're eating and how it was grown—of course, beans are preferred to beef, even if the beef came from a farm down the street—but how far it traveled? Doesn't matter.

It matters, though, for things such as local economies, the maintenance of cultural tradition and regional foodways, and the simple matter of the sense of community that comes from going to the farmers' market or knowing that the apples you picked up at a grocery store didn't spend days or weeks on a truck or ship. Here in Puerto Rico, where famously 85 percent of food is imported, why would I want onions from California that are already going moldy in the grocery store when I can get flavorful, fresh ones by supporting a local farmer?[24] Or buy imported eggs in a supermarket instead of local ones, whose prices aren't as affected by global inflation? Numbers aren't all that matter when we're talking about the food system, because the quality of the ingredients we're cooking with and the good feeling of talking to the person who grew those ingredients aren't really quantifiable.

Why wouldn't we want to move toward smaller farms and prioritizing local economies? I would prefer to buy my pens from my local pharmacy than order them on Amazon, because one of these contributes to my neighborhood and the other union-busts and underpays its own employees, who've worked hard enough over the years to help the founder Jeff Bezos fly to space for some reason. The same principle stands when it comes to food: Why would I support massive agricultural and biotech conglomerates who underpay workers and also don't pay the real environmental cost of their pesticide-heavy, monocrop practices instead of supporting my local community?

Vandana Shiva, in *Mold* magazine, said, "Abundance is where the seed and the food are interconnected again. Instead of eating 10,000 kinds of plants appropriate to place, and creating living economies appropriate to place, we made eating the ultimate act of alienation from the earth."[25] "Appropriate to place" is the key phrase here, which is precisely why it's a terrible though predictable fact that the local food movement in the US has been made into a bourgeois joke.

Food-policy journalist Lisa Held took this idea to task in her newsletter *Peeled*, writing, "In the face of dire climate predictions, it can be tempting to rank straight emissions above all other concerns, but saying that local food is 'not better for the climate' solely on the basis that there's no definitive proof that miles matter much, without considering any other factors, is jumping to a conclusion."[26]

A food product's significance and impact have to be determined in the aggregate, by looking at how they're affecting the health of not just the soil and surrounding water but the workers toiling to bring it to people's tables. As Held concludes, farms that work on a smaller scale to sell to their local markets are going to minimize poor environmental and human effects by the very virtue of their work. If you're not trying to feed the whole country, you're not going to produce at a scale that creates waste, taxes the soil, uses excessive water, or gets packaged in plastic and Styrofoam to make long trips while remaining intact.

I return egg cartons and plastic pint containers for cherry tomatoes to our farmers' market each week, because I know they'll be reused. I use any plastic produce bags to pick up dog poop. These are the rhythm of my week, in sync with my market. Do I sound elitist for these practices?

For some reason, Lappé was excellent at conveying her points without alienating people—she was inviting; she was rooted in fact and not aesthetics. This is her legacy: shifting the food narrative for the white middle class.

But the farm-to-table movement that emerged in the early twenty-first century was swiftly slapped down as elitist. Its "high priests," as a 2013 op-ed by Henry I. Miller and Jayson Lusk referred to them, were Michael Pollan, author of *The Omnivore's Dilemma*, chef and activist Alice Waters of Berkeley's Chez Panisse, and writer Mark Bittman.[27] Miller and Lusk's op-ed comes from a free-market perspective in which all that really matters is the efficiency and cost of production; ecological concerns aren't a factor, and if local produce really does taste better, then it should have no problem selling at a high, unsubsidized cost.

By anointing "high priests" and priestesses who all looked and sounded quite similar to each other, the media easily made a mockery of the food movement in the United States. While the 1970s seemed full of hope, the lack of a big, broad, diverse coalition to keep pressure on the government has meant taxpayer money subsidizes industrial meat and dairy at a rate of $38 billion per year.[28] During the COVID-19 pandemic, nearly sixty thousand cases were traced back to meatpacking workers in unsafe conditions.[29] When a fake news story went viral about President Joe Biden limiting people's beef consumption to four pounds per year, there was outrage on the part of omnivores, who posted gigantic steaks on social media in protest. All of this could make a person very pessimistic.

At this crucial moment in the life of this planet, though, there is no time for that. We've known—all these people have known and do know—that the Global North sucks resources from the Global South, deforests it, demands cheap goods from it, and that fight has only become more fierce with the experience of a global pandemic. Here could be where we change, where we radically alter our relationship to fossil fuels and mindless consumption. First, though, we need to understand how meat came to obtain its vaunted status, its platinum-standard cultural capital, to the point that it is destroying the planet. Then we'll get back to how people have tried and are trying to change that.

2. MEAT'S MEANING

U pton Sinclair dedicated his 1906 novel *The Jungle* to "the work-
ingmen of America." Sinclair was a socialist, and he wanted to
let his fellow countrypeople know that the conditions workers were
suffering in the meat-processing industry were unconscionable. The
effect this novel actually had, though, was to make people concerned
about the safety of *consuming* meat processed in terrible working
conditions. No one wanted disease in their steak, of course, but the
person doing the slaughtering and breaking down of the whole cow?
Well, a job is a job.

Despite *The Jungle* often being required reading for American
schoolchildren, and despite roughly fifty years of mainstream conversation about the ill health and environmental effects of the meat-based
American diet, little has changed about the labor of meat processing.
It is still a very poorly paid, very dangerous job. In the COVID-19
pandemic, that danger increased exponentially. Tyson, the largest
producer of chicken in the US, has concentrated power in Arkansas,
where it is the third biggest employer. According to reporting by *The
Guardian*, it advertises jobs as paying fifteen dollars per hour that don't
actually exist, and workers who've been there for over twenty years
are paid just fourteen dollars per hour, while their benefits have been
slashed, their speed is documented to the detriment of food safety,
and there were not enough precautions taken to inhibit the spread of

COVID-19: 13 percent of its workforce in Arkansas had contracted the virus as of June 2021.[1]

About 40 percent of the meat-processing workers in the United States are immigrants, of whom about 14 percent are undocumented, and thus without even the bare minimum of state protection to safeguard them against poor working conditions and pay.[2] As Alice Driver reported for the *New York Review of Books*, a worker at a Tyson plant in Arkansas named Plácido Leopoldo Arrue died of COVID-19. His widow also told Driver about the lung damage he suffered in a work accident in 2011, when he inhaled a chlorine gas originally developed as a chemical weapon in World War I now being used as a bleach on chicken parts.[3] Abuses in the industry have been ongoing. A 2019 Human Rights Watch report titled *"When We're Dead and Buried, Our Bones Will Keep Hurting": Workers' Rights Under Threat in US Meat and Poultry Plants* noted, among other horrors, that "between 2013 and 2017, 8 workers died, on average, each year because of an incident in their plant."[4]

If we could remind people who eat industrially produced meat that the workers, the people, are suffering, they will start to care. They will change their habits. They will understand that so much meat cannot be produced so cheaply without horrifying labor conditions. I stop talking about the greenhouse gas emissions; I don't mention animal rights. But then I remember that Upton Sinclair tried this over a hundred years ago, and I don't know whether people have changed enough to have a different reaction.

Most of us in the United States grow up believing meat is an inevitable and undeniable part of our diets, a birthright, and that its production—the slaughter necessary to make it available—can and should be invisible if that is what is required to make sure nothing about its abundance changes. Making sure meat feels as essential as air is part of the American project, because meat means everything in the United States. Masculine virility, affluence, and white cowboys overtaking the plains have long been key elements of the American imaginary, and they are what meat—specifically beef—represents culturally and politically. It's that connection to American identity that leads people to shout and shut their ears when any of the horrors of meat productions are noted, much like the killing of Indigenous peoples has been made invisible in the national narrative. It's that connection that saw President Donald Trump declaring meat processing "critical infrastructure" at the start of the coronavirus pandemic, without ensuring workers would be safe or even compensated for working at such incredible risk to their health. Between April 2020 and April 2021, nearly sixty thousand meatpacking workers became infected with the virus.[5] We will stop at nothing to keep meat plentiful, even going so far as to create fake burgers that bleed.

A common refrain among right-wingers is that the Democrats (never mind their own center-right policies that wouldn't dare get in the way of industrial meat and dairy's lobbyists) will take away their hamburgers. That challenge came to a head in April 2021 when the *Daily Mail* ran a false story about President Biden's climate plan; from this piece, it was extrapolated that each person in the US would only be able to consume four pounds of beef per year.[6] From there, a group of mainly men went wild on Twitter, posting pictures of their giant steaks: some well-cooked, others monstrosities. They couldn't fathom a life without regular beef. And why would they?

Consider the advertisements for beef and pork that were so popular in the 1980s and 1990s, funded with taxpayer money through what's called a "commodity checkoff program" that allows taxes paid on these commodities to go into research and marketing.[7] These checkoff programs must promote themselves in a generic manner only, not tell people to buy from a specific brand. Thus, "Beef. It's What's for Dinner," and "Pork. The Other White Meat" were refrains that were drilled into my head in childhood, spoken by strong male voices. "The Incredible, Edible Egg" and "Got Milk?" were other refrains. There's an obvious pattern here, right? Animal products had and continue to have the most money behind them. Meat, eggs, and dairy milk have their production subsidized by the federal government at $38 billion per year, and somehow the animal reality of their origin has been rendered invisible, becoming what the vegan scholar Carol J. Adams calls the "absent referent" in her 1990 book *The Sexual Politics of Meat*.

When a vegetable goes mainstream, though, that's when people are puzzled. That happened in the beginning of the 2010s, when kale suddenly had a moment of popularity. The NPR program *All Things Considered* asked in 2013, "What Elevated Kale from Vegetable to Cultural Identifier?"[8] Reporter Dan Bobkoff noticed kale stickers, kale T-shirts—I had one of those at the time, and even occasional vegan Beyoncé wore a sweatshirt emblazoned with "KALE" in the video for the song "7/11" in 2014—and wanted to know, "Why do some people see kale as a part of their identities?" Imagine the same question asked of meat on National Public Radio—it just wouldn't happen. But kale, a nutritious, hearty, and versatile green: its popularity was mysterious.

Though the truth was, kale had become popular in a pretty mysterious way. One story that was repeated in the media claimed the American Kale Association had hired a public relations firm more famous for fashion campaigns to promote the vegetable. That association doesn't actually exist, though—it was the PR company's founder, a woman named Oberon Sinclair, who had taken it upon herself to do a publicity stunt on the vegetable's behalf in 2015. In truth, the green had already been growing in popularity. What Google Trends shows is that kale started to gain more traction in 2004, indeed peaked in 2014 when Beyoncé wore the word "KALE" on a sweatshirt, and has been a steadily popular search term ever since. Many people hate kale but more of us swear by it.

The interesting thing is that to create the fake American Kale Association, Sinclair copied the practices of the meat and dairy checkoff programs in service to a vegetable.[9] There is no kale lobby, yet its sudden popularity in the early 2010s made a lot of people curious, and we in the US have become accustomed to our trends being governed solely by money. A kale lobby was a plausible idea, when in fact, it was organic growth that explained kale's surge in popularity. Beef's market dominance is the story that's actually been manufactured.

~⁓

Indeed, beef is considered more American than fried chicken, apple pie, and turkey on Thanksgiving. Beef means steak, it means hamburgers: the two most rugged cowboy meals imaginable. And it has always been political. Settler colonialism, the term that describes the displacement of Indigenous peoples in favor of European settlers, was essential to the creation of the beef industry—as it was for many other beloved American institutions. Nineteenth-century government policy saw the Great Plains ecosystem turned from a grass-bison-nomad system to a grass-cattle-rancher one, with the Indian Wars a necessary step in the establishment of the rancher mythos. Bison herds were decimated as a practice by settlers who saw them as "monstrous," according to Joshua Specht's book *Red Meat Republic: A Hoof-to-Table History of How Beef Changed America*, with cattle representing civilization. Along with those herds also went the communities that depended on hunting them for survival. "Cattle ranchers and bison hunters, supported by the U.S. military, fundamentally reshaped the Great Plains," writes Specht, "expelling American Indians from western lands and appropriating that land for use by white settlers and ranchers."[10] Without this process of extermination and colonization, he says, beef's emergence as a staple of the American diet might not have occurred so readily.

People in the US are eating less beef lately, though, likely because of its bad press regarding its greenhouse gas emissions and poor health outcomes around heart health. Those people who aren't eating as much beef aren't switching to vegetarianism; they're just eating more chicken. In 2020, the most consumed meat in the US was "broiler chicken" (meaning any chicken born and bred for consumption), clocking in at 95.4 pounds per capita. That number is expected to increase to 96.4 pounds in 2029.[11] Chicken's reputation as "good" for the climate is only by comparison to beef, because its greenhouse gas emissions per serving are still eleven times higher than that of beans.[12] Still, this shows some impact regarding messaging—it just didn't land on the side of beans, but it's still progress, sort of, if you don't think about all those Tyson workers getting sick during the pandemic, suffering repetitive motion injuries, and being paid a less than livable wage.

There's plenty of reason for concern, because while the US is consuming slightly less beef, letting chicken outrun it in sales, the rest of the world is now getting a taste for cheap cow (as well as pork). According to a report by *Global Meat & Poultry Trends*, meat consumption around the globe is expected to increase by 1.4 percent in 2023, with poultry accounting for 47 percent of the meat market by 2031.[13] This isn't something the planet can handle. The European Union, Japan, the UK, and the US have pledged to hit net-zero emissions by 2050 to stave off total climate disaster—itself the true bare minimum of a goal, far off and too late. Would that change how we eat? Yes, which is why so many people in the US are committed to meat's significance, no matter the cost.

Biden really had and has no plan for climate change that will curb meat consumption in any real way, unlike what was falsely reported by the *Daily Mail*. But that will not stop people from losing their minds over the idea that someone, somewhere is trying to force-feed them vegetables in lieu of juicy flesh. This constant anxiety about vegetarianism, which is understood as feminine, comes out in myriad ways and strikes at basically every cuisine on the planet. Taking away meat means taking away autonomy, virility, and cultural meaning, many argue. This posturing, which also exists in "real life" contexts, takes on new meaning as performance when it happens on social media, where the only way of building a self is to amplify every concern to the point of parody. Here, the meat obsessives take their need for real animal meat to new heights of absurdity to ensure everyone reading is aware of their masculine rejection of vegetables.

We were approaching one year of being stuck inside because of the COVID-19 pandemic when a tweet went viral: "I will never unsee this absolutely horrifying vegan al pastor," said a Los Angeles–based journalist.[14] The accompanying photo was a brown and green mass of mushroom and nopales dotted with red spice made by Evil Cooks, meant to be a vegetable-based take on classic Mexican al pastor, usually made with pork.

Most of the response validated the original critique, with many people calling vegetables disgusting and meat a natural thing to eat. Others said that vegans want to eat meat so badly and shouldn't make anything that resembles it if they don't want to kill animals for their meals.

What's interesting is that al pastor is a tradition born of immigration, of cultural fusion and influence from Lebanese people who'd moved to Puebla and modeled it after their own famous lamb dish: shawarma. Al pastor tacos were even originally called "tacos árabes." Couldn't the use of vegetables represent another stage in that evolution? A necessary one toward meat not being at the center of each and every meal?

"Growing up, visiting taco shops on the weekend was my family's religion, more so even than Catholicism," writer Andrea Aliseda tells me.[15] She grew up in Tijuana, Mexico, eating carne asada and al pastor tacos, competing with her brother to see who could eat more. In the years since, she's become vegan, and after that viral tweet, she went to try the vegan al pastor herself.

"I studied the *trompo*, waiting for the moment when I'd see the *taquero*, Alex, carve out my tacos," Aliseda says. A *trompo* is the vertical broiler on which pastor (and shawarma) are made. "The experience was incredibly satisfying. It took me back to being a kid, watching the *taqueros* move with quickness and precision." The vegan al pastor was constructed with layers of mushroom, cabbage, eggplant, and onion. Aliseda grew up with a different type of al pastor that was red, while the one Evil Cooks was selling was black, made with the *recado negro* marinade from Yucatán. Having Aliseda explain the differences made it more interesting, because I had heard from others that the color was "wrong," not simply a regional expression.

Such claims about "authenticity" are something vegans from non-Western cultures struggle with, because even while much pre-Columbian cuisine in Mexico was plant-based, meat has become central to the idea of the major foods for many. "There's this sentiment that you're not Mexican if you're vegan," Aliseda says.

The criticisms and vocalizations of disgust on Twitter against the vegan al pastor were validated by a piece published the same week in the *New Republic*, in which vegan scholars Jan Dutkiewicz and Gabriel N. Rosenberg argued that the cuisine of meatless eaters had too long been ascetic and unappealing.[16] It was only with the advent of lab and tech meat, either made from the cells of animals or through soy and pea protein, that people could be expected to convert to vegetarianism en masse, the academic authors argued. And they have supporters in the culinary world and beyond: the Impossible Burger launched itself with chef partnerships, working with folks such as David Chang, a previously vocal anti-vegetarian, and has now landed on menus at Burger Kings, as noted, as well as at White Castles and Little Caesars across the nation.[17] These aren't spaces known for a vegetarian-friendly ethos. Tad Friend, writing in the *New Yorker* on tech meat, referred to "the pallid satisfactions of bean sprouts and quinoa."[18] One might accuse the rest of the American populace of contenting itself with the climate-destroying flesh of kind cows, but the more significant issue that this brings to light is how meatless food has been, and continues to be, a bland joke.

All of this acts to justify the role of meat in society, despite its historical meaning as a representation of masculine virility and current status as a planet destroyer. There can be no life without meat, both the omnivores and lab meat apologists say. They focus on a taste, that of all meats, is seemingly impossible to give up, and cite only the thinking of men like Peter Singer and Robert Nozick. Singer is famously a "utilitarian," and these arguments are in line with his thinking: cell and tech meat performs a function, one that some have deemed necessary, without considering the land impacts of defor- estation to grow monocropped GMO soy for Impossible Burgers, a lack of biodiversity for the Beyond Burger's pea protein, and global cultural traditions that are based on localized meat instead of the US's 220 pounds per year of industrial meat per person.

These conditions of meat dependence created for the US are not natural, which is where the veggie burger haters lose me.

In his book *The Meat Question: Animals, Humans, and the Deep History of Food*, Josh Berson argues that meat did not actually play a pivotal role in human evolution, but that evolution "did facilitate a greater opportunistic reliance on meat."[19] Affluence in a country like China, which has historically not relied on meat as a centerpiece of its style of cooking, has led to it being a major importer of beef from places like Australia, Brazil, and Uruguay. So much so that now the new tech meat makers are focusing their sights on Asia, despite the continent's long history with non-animal proteins like tofu, tempeh, seitan, and chickpeas. This is technologically based cultural imperi- alism, driven by capital.

Eat Just, which makes an egg-like product, and Impossible Foods, which uses GMO soy in its fake red meat, made major moves into the Asian market in 2020. The former set up a facility in Singapore, where it will be investing $20 million, and the latter is now available directly to consumers at grocery stores in Hong Kong and Singa- pore.[20] Upon the announcement of the new facility, Eat Just sent out a press release saying the new space will "generate thousands of metric tons of protein."[21] What a dystopian way to speak of food, and a clear representation of how well aligned this sector is with its cattle baron predecessors in the United States.

Much of the new lab and tech meat, as well as other "plant-based" products, in form and function, harken back to the early days of the meat industry as we now know it in the US. This replication owes to the reliance on the same cultural ideas and industrial structures, with the new addition of climate considerations. The amount of money poured into the development of these products is akin to the subsidies that make industrial meat so excessively abundant.

Aleph Farms in Tel Aviv, Israel, debuted a 3D-printed steak in 2021 after raising $12 million in 2019.[22] The Impossible Foods burger cost $80 million to develop. Beyond Meat's IPO debuted with a $1.5 billion valuation. This is about money, not saving the planet and not creating new conditions and models for the economy and consumption. They're banking on making their products invaluable, with the help of greenwashing. According to Marco Springmann, senior environmental researcher at the University of Oxford, the tech burgers at fast-food restaurants have a carbon footprint that is five times that of a veggie burger made with legumes and grains.[23] Findings also show that meat made in a lab would, over time, not stabilize warming and emissions as well as low consumption of beef.[24] Nothing about these newfangled products is all that much better for the planet: it's just better for some people's pockets.

Impossible and Beyond, by coming onto the market with burgers, have focused on fast food to sell their products without demanding any changes in their other operating procedures: the fast-food places still sell questionably sourced meat and dairy; their workers are still not paid enough to live. What bold new future is this? It sounds precisely like the past.

I don't discount the significance of these products as a stopgap measure, if indeed people are willing to choose them over meat burgers every time. The issue, for me, begins with their positioning themselves as a "solution" to climate change—not a stop on the way toward a future where land used to grow grain to feed livestock is returned to its Indigenous peoples and poverty has been eradicated, but the continuation of capitalist modes of production in which companies and their shareholders receive the bulk of the profits, use land for their purposes, and force workers in their factories and at restaurants serving their products to remain in their class position. They reject words like "vegan" or "vegetarian" in their marketing, as well, opting for the ultimately more malleable phrase "plant-based"—which can sometimes mean vegan, can sometimes mean the use of egg, can sometimes signify a dish that's mostly vegetables and grains but is also topped with salmon. I've consistently wondered why vegans like to defend these products when the marketers refuse to acknowledge that many people have long subsisted on seitan and beans for protein.

These companies are certainly not marketing to those who have given up meat. Indeed, no vegetarian or vegan I've ever met—I'm speaking anecdotally here—wants to eat these. Now when you recommend a veggie burger to vegetarians, they ask, "Is it a real veggie burger?" "Real," meaning, is it made from legumes, grains, and vegetables? Is it recognizable as food, or is it pretending to be beef? The latter has been the selling point for the so-called plant-based meats, while for Impossible Foods the bigger selling point has been their proprietary product, "heme."

Heme, in meat, is in the protein hemoglobin in an animal's blood or myoglobin in the muscle, which is believed to give hamburgers their color and slightly metallic flavor. In the Impossible Foods version, the DNA of soy plants is inserted into a genetically engineered yeast and then fermented. This results in both the pink color and "blood" of their patties, which have been greeted as a planet-saving miracle by the mainstream press and are now in every Burger King in the United States.

Impossible Foods seems to have created heme out of a belief that it's the visual simulation of blood oozing from a burger that gives it an addictive taste. Why would anyone want tofu, seitan, or tempeh if it doesn't bleed? What good is a veggie burger made from beans, rice, and carrots when a patty could come fully formed off the assembly line looking eerily like cow flesh?

In her book *Meathooked: The History and Science of Our 2.5-Million-Year Obsession with Meat*, writer Marta Zaraska looks at why human beings have not been able to stop eating meat, despite evidence of its disastrous effects on the climate and our health. She explores how meat has long been a status symbol—in gender, class, and even nationalism. "Our relationship to meat is powerful," Zaraska writes, and that's why our books and films and advertisements use meat analogues so widely and eagerly: if you remove this symbol, you have to make up the difference somehow.[25] When you're no longer exerting power over animals, it helps to at least look like you could, and to eat food that resembles flesh.

It's not surprising, then, who is most attached to the consumption of animals: "Recent scientific studies confirm that those of us who hold authoritarian beliefs, who think social hierarchy is important, who seek wealth and power and support human dominance over nature, eat more meat than those who stand against inequality," Zaraska writes.

Zaraska, a vegetarian, is pragmatic (and somewhat pessimistic) in her thoughts on why the movement against meat consumption can't write new rules—why it adopts products backed by venture capital and developed for fast food. "In a perfect world, we wouldn't need to advertise vegetarianism or veganism by using old cultural stereotypes and clichés; we wouldn't need to emphasize that vegetarian men are still masculine and powerful, and so on," she told me over email. "But we don't live in a perfect world, and sometimes it's better to play on these cultural stereotypes and the old symbolism of meat to encourage people to slowly change their ways and reduce meat consumption. Then, maybe, in the future, we will be able to completely forgo that historical heritage, forget that meat used to symbolize power over . . . nature, over the poor, over women. But we are not there yet, not even close."[26]

And so beef's hold, especially, remains. Through the concentration of capital at the Chicago meatpackers and their political ties, to today's tech meat patties, mimicking that which they hope to replace, beef's significance as a symbol has not loosened a bit despite the devastating truth of its impact on the environment and the fact that the current success of imitations may lead to similar issues because of monocropping, centralized production, and singular supply chains.

Another tried-and-true American tradition is fast food, which has long been a symbol of American imperialism and conquest itself, and that's why Impossible Foods and Beyond Meat make such a perfect pairing with Burger King, White Castle, and their ilk. All are profit-driven, corporate enterprises built upon the central tenet of capitalism: endless growth. Never mind that that pursuit has been a clear cause of environmental destruction. Even without actual beef, how does a corporate tech-faux-meat patty manufactured from genetically modified soy protein, served by underpaid labor and likely garnished with a tomato picked by a slave-wage worker and on a bun made of GMO wheat flour, truly change the system that beef built?

These products are no longer the juggernauts they once were and their alliance with fast food has failed, for now. Beyond Meat went public on the stock market in May 2019 and its share price increased 163 percent on the first day of trading.[27] The share price has since decreased wildly, with sales of plant-based meats overall decreasing 0.5 percent in 2021.[28] The boom has slowed, with Burger King cutting the price of its Impossible Whopper in hopes of increasing sales, and various new products like Beyond Fried Chicken at KFC and a Beyond Meat "McPlant" at McDonald's both flopping with diners.[29] Global meat consumption is expected to increase 14 percent by 2030.[30] This is a loss for these companies and a win for industrial animal agriculture, but it shouldn't be interpreted as a total loss when there is still room to change behavior through policy and a resurgent focus on sustainable proteins such as legumes, tofu, and tempeh.

Veggie burgers can still be made from locally sourced vegetables and a diversity of grains and legumes that come from a varied supply chain. Old-school patties, with their recognizable lists of ingredients, can rise to burger supremacy once again. The willful mistakes of the beef industry that have been so deeply damaging to the environment, workers, and cows alike don't have to be replicated in a new fashion, supported once again by government subsidies and consumerism. Supporting biodiversity and locality can be understood as a tenet of the plant-based lifestyle, one that considers a broader understanding of sustainability, ethics, and compassion. It can't start and stop with the consumption of animal products: the effects of food on the land, on workers, and on the culture at large must be taken into account.

Beef—real and tech—does not do this. It invites consumers to expand their palates and politics only a bit, only to the extent that corporations are still making a profit, soy and pea protein rule the marketplace, and little must shift about how one views their relationship to food and the earth: *Eat this burger patty, which is just like what you already know, because it's better for the planet* (so they say). *Ask no further questions.* A vegetarian perspective—if it truly cares for people and planet—demands more, or could. Often, I talk to the founders of venture capital–backed agri-tech firms developing new food technologies and they speak of the lack of imagination in most of the populace, and how they can capitalize on that. Instead of redefining what a burger is, what ice cream tastes like, or what the texture of cheese should be in a way that relies more on biodiversity, human ingenuity, and relationships with animals that don't regard them solely as bodies to be used, these growth-minded capitalists want to see as little change as possible in order to continue greenwashing corporate motivations.

Because I gave meat up willingly and easily, the desire to continue eating anything that replicates its flavors and textures mystifies me perhaps a bit too much. Conversations with more casual vegetarians lead me to believe that these tech burgers scratch at an itch a traditional veggie burger cannot. I understand them a bit when I bite into the tofu-fried tofu sandwich (also known as the TFT) at Superiority Burger: here, the crispy organic tofu from Hodo Soy topped with slaw and a spicy spread satisfies my desire for fried chicken. But if anyone pretended it wasn't tofu, I wouldn't want to eat it. You could even call it "chik'n," as many vegan products do, and it would be depressing to me—a vegan food searching for the flavor language of death and decay. I want to leave industrialized meat and all the sadness and destruction it has caused the planet in my past, in everyone's past. This requires maybe too much change, too much sacrifice.

Those of us who've already given up meat, though, have a blueprint for how to combine concern for what is on our plates with what is happening politically, socially, and economically. Through zines, grassroots organizing, and even restaurants, vegetarianism and veganism have been developing as a malleable means of responding to oppression in all its forms. Beef has a stranglehold on the US culinary landscape, on the cultural and culinary language we speak, but that can change with resistance to the new corporate tech meat. By taking a broad interest in a plant-based diet for the sake of climate change and showing folks how sustainability means more than just making adjustments to fast-food orders, the US food system could wake up to a brand-new day. But it will require taking culture, gastronomy, and taste into consideration, not just ethics.

3. FOUNDATIONS OF A NEW AMERICAN CUISINE

The soybean has long been used as a symbol of "alternative" food in the United States because of its strong association with 1970s counterculture cuisine, an offshoot of the counterculture fore-grounded by anti–Vietnam War activism. From this, a natural foods movement became possible. Yet it's actually what we could call an "establishment crop": soy farming, like industrial meat and dairy production, is heavily subsidized by the government, and just over 70 percent of the soybeans grown in the US are fed to livestock.[1] As of 2018, 94 percent of all soy grown in the US was genetically modified, and it is regarded as one of the "big 8" allergens, though it has the lowest prevalence, showing up in about three of every one thousand adults.[2]

The reputation and understanding of soy in the US began in the early twentieth century. The initial intention of scientists at the USDA when they were looking to diversify the crops in the American South at the start of the twentieth century was a good one: they were eyeing soybeans because they knew that using land to grow only cotton—monocropping—was bad for the soil's health and lon-gevity. Some even noted that as meat was becoming more expensive for the American worker, soy protein could serve as a replacement. What happened instead is that the soy became livestock feed, keeping meat cheap. Even those red-blooded American men who posted their massive steaks upon hearing that the website Epicurious would stop publishing new beef recipes in 2021 are thus eating quite a bit of soy. It's the American way: tofu by way of cattle.

Despite many people's best efforts, though, soy foods that tout their soy-ness have remained niche, even if they have been quite profitable at certain times in the last fifty years. It would seem tofu, tempeh, and other plant-based traditional proteins that have roots in Asian cuisines are at a pivotal juncture, as a great deal of media attention, venture capital, and research money is poured into a new wave of tech and lab meat products that are decidedly more recognizable to those who are accustomed to ingesting soy only through the intermediary of a cow's flesh.

My first time eating tofu was at the neighborhood Japanese restaurant in Patchogue, where I grew up on Long Island. Its name was Heisei; today, the land on which it once stood is home to a Walgreens. The white cubes of silken bean curd floated in the salty miso soup that came as an appetizer to my entrée—I always ordered shrimp tempura or teriyaki, never sushi—and eating it made me feel worldly. Sometimes I'd ask for extra in my bowl, not understanding that it was likely pre-made, and was nonetheless accommodated by the kitchen staff who were likely cursing me. We were regulars, my parents always ordering both sushi and sashimi; my dad always asking for both soup and a salad dressed in carrot and ginger. The fountain Cokes there were more syrup than soda, and I'll never forget the taste. Tofu and Coca-Cola—an American diet for a suburban kid in the '90s.

Tofu became something I ate only as itself, when having Japanese or Chinese food, or stuffed into a cold salad wrap at a more hippie-dippy restaurant when I got a little older. Nowadays, I can't resist a block of it that's been marinated, battered, and deep-fried, drenched in hot sauce or just stuffed on a bun with slaw, like the tofu-fried tofu at Superiority Burger. But what I really want is mapo tofu, sans pork, spicy and numbing. I'm bad at cooking tofu myself, too impatient to press it, marinate it, and give it time in the cast-iron. Really good tofu still tastes like a treat to me, a special meal only to be had outside the house. When I do manage to cook up a good batch at home, I consider the feat a culinary victory.

It was the only traditional plant-based protein that I consumed first in a way in which it was intended to be eaten, with its cultural context intact. I ate seitan at Foodswings, which was a restaurant in Williamsburg, Brooklyn (now a natural wine bar), and tempeh at Angelica Kitchen, an organic vegan restaurant that was open for forty years (now a nondescript restaurant). My friend from high school, Candice, had been vegetarian and then vegan, and when I was beginning my own meatless journey, we went to Angelica Kitchen; it was there that I found out that tempeh might indeed be my favorite plant protein, so funky and mushroomy. "Fermented" became a key word in my vegan transition, as I realized that was the way toward umami that was so often missing in plant-based food, if you didn't actively seek it out. Candice had also taken me once to Foodswings, probably when we were going to a concert; I'd heard so much about their tofu buffalo wings, which looked more like breaded chicken cutlets on a stick dipped in hot sauce. I longed to enjoy the food at this place, because to me, it seemed so cool, but the seitan gyro I ordered reached into the uncanny valley—was it meat or wasn't it?—and I couldn't finish it.

These were two important vegan restaurants in New York City that nonetheless represented very different subcultures: the hippie at Angelica Kitchen and the punk at Foodswings. When I talk about traditional proteins, too, I see these restaurants as the icons of various meatless approaches to building a unique gastronomy in the United States. Tofu became popular in the '70s, and tempeh and seitan followed, to varying levels of success. Some uses were traditional to their various origins in Asia; others were American inventions—like, for example, tofu buffalo wings, seitan gyros, and tempeh Reubens—causing a severing from their source.

Those sources were all different. Tofu originated in China, first mentioned in the year 965 CE in a document called the *Qing Yilu* by Tao Ku. It's referred to as "the vice mayor's mutton," in reference to a vice mayor who was so poor that he could only eat this soybean cake rather than mutton. It's understood that tofu—written as *doufu* in Mandarin, which became *tofu* in Japanese—was an inexpensive protein widely consumed by the poor. English-language writings would start to mention it in the 1700s, as a nutritious "curd" or cheese; the first commercial tofu-maker on record in the Western world is Wo Sing & Co., which opened in San Francisco in 1878. The number of tofu shops would steadily rise, and by 1950, there were at least 425, mainly owned by Japanese people serving their own communities and geographically concentrated on the West Coast.[3]

Seitan, in the form it is known today, came about during the macrobiotic diet craze of the 1960s. It was developed by Kiyoshi Mokutani, a student of George Ohsawa—important figures in pushing the macrobiotic style of eating—who coined the term that puts together the Japanese words for "fresh" (*sei*) and "protein" (*tanpaku*). It made its way to the West in 1969, via the Erewhon natural foods company—it still has shops in California. But extracting gluten from wheat for food has much earlier origins in China, as a meat substitute developed for Buddhists practicing strict vegetarian diets. In Japan, wheat gluten used as a protein source for Buddhists was called "*fu*." For the most part, the word "seitan" has stayed in use only in the West and in macrobiotic circles.[4]

Tempeh, the third major plant protein to become deeply associated with vegetarian and vegan diets in the West, originated in Indonesia in the 1600s, where soybeans left in a banana leaf fermented thanks to a specific bacteria, *Rhizopus oligosporus*, which formed an edible mycelium between the beans, creating the cake-like tempeh we now know that gets turned most often into a cured meat substitute because of its rich flavor and mutability: bacon in a BLT, corned beef in a Reuben. It can be made from myriad combinations of legumes and grains, but the environment for fermentation must be strictly controlled.

Often, bigger companies pasteurize the tempeh to give it a longer shelf-life in refrigerators, but for me, nothing compares to fresh tempeh sold and kept frozen, all its mushroomy glory intact, and most who've compared types or made it themselves would agree. But it's a lot of work.

The beans are soaked twice before they are ready to cook; they're then pulsed in a blender until they're about a quarter of the size they once were. After this they're cooked until underdone to keep the moisture level low, giving the culture space to grow. You then drain the beans and dry them with a fan or hair dryer, until they're just damp. Finally, you stir them up with the separate bacterial culture, usually purchased, divide the mix into bags, and put them into an incubator.

The temperature has to stay between 80 and 90 degrees. If it gets too hot, you'll kill the culture. If done correctly, though, black spots will sprout around the holes in the bag where air has been allowed in, a thick, white mycelium will have formed between the beans, and—twenty-four to thirty-two hours later—the tempeh is ready to be cooked or frozen.

Commercial production is equally as intense. In 2015, I met with Barry Schwartz, who makes the New York City–based Barry's Tempeh, to watch the process. At the production kitchen in Long Island City, Schwartz and his team are just doing a bigger version of this, using bread proofers as incubators and a laundromat-style centrifuge in lieu of a hair dryer.

There are other regional producers of fresh tempeh, like Smiling Hara in Asheville, North Carolina, which suffered a recall in 2012 because of a salmonella outbreak. (Apparently, many people didn't realize that tempeh cannot be eaten raw.) Twin Oaks, an intentional community in Virginia, sells its own; the Bay Area, of course, has its producers. One maker in Puerto Rico uses a base of garbanzo. It's very concentrated, though, and because all of these makers are promoted differently and locally, fresh tempeh stays a somewhat underground obsession.

People have come from all over the world to stay with Schwartz— who got started as a cook when he lived on an ashram—and learn the process, so that they can take it to new places and maybe make tempeh with whichever grains and legumes are abundant in specific regions. When I spent a year intermittently observing the Barry's Tempeh business, someone from Toronto had stayed with him in anticipation of starting his own operation, and Schwartz had been in conversations with a doctor in Maryland who wanted to make tempeh in Dubai. It's an apprentice style of learning, one that reminds me of how these soy proteins became popularized outside of their original cultural contexts.

To untangle how these three proteins became the foundations and symbols of vegetarian and vegan eating in the US, we have to travel from California to Japan with William Shurtleff, who would meet the illustrator Akiko Aoyagi in Tokyo and write texts on tofu, tempeh, miso, and more that continue to be the most extensive resources on the history of these foods available in English.

Though tofu was being made for retail sale in the United States since at least 1878, Shurtleff and Aoyagi are credited with setting off a boom by making the tofu-making process, history, and related recipes accessible to a Western audience. Between 1976 and 1981, the number of tofu-makers in the US tripled.

Shurtleff and Aoyagi came together in the early 1970s in Tokyo, where they began doing research into soy foods throughout Asia. It was *The Book of Tofu* that was their big debut and biggest success in 1975, and for which they studied closely with traditional tofu-makers in Japan. They'd go on to write *The Book of Miso* and *The Book of Tempeh*, as well as put together a deep archive of soy's global history at the SoyInfo Center, which they founded in 1976. Much like Frances Moore Lappé did with *Diet for a Small Planet*, they normalized the idea of using plants for protein rather than animals, for readers who hadn't been exposed to this idea and had no framework for it, no understanding of how to change their habits at the grocery store or in the kitchen. All these books included many recipes, for that reason.

It helped, of course, that Shurtleff was a white man from California, inspired by Lappé's work. Interviews about *The Book of Tofu* published upon its release focused mainly on Shurtleff, with *Mother Earth News* noting Aoyagi's "delightfully accented English."[5] This makes sense: up until the '70s tofu had been considered "too foreign," as Jia-Chen Fu, a professor at Emory University, told the magazine *Inverse* in 2021.[6] (Though it had also been beloved by Seventh-Day Adventists—nearly 30 percent of whom are vegetarian—early in the twentieth century, who used it to create cheese products and canned bologna.)[7]

With the new dawn of natural foods in the US beginning in the 1960s, the reputation of soy as something foreign or simply strange changed, and tofu gradually became a go-to for both health and environmental reasons in certain circles. The Farm commune's cookbook, published in 1975, relies on soy in all forms, from milk to tofu to yuba to tempeh, placing these "hippies" at the vanguard of vegan eating in the US. David Mintz's launch of Tofutti ice cream in the '80s started to normalize non-dairy dairy products, and Tofurky—the roast popular at vegetarian Thanksgivings—would be introduced to the market in 1995 by Turtle Island Foods.[8] Soy milk, until being unseated by almond and eventually oat, was the alternative milk of choice, peaking in 2008 as a $1.2 billion industry.[9]

Soy food products haven't been without their controversies, however. Racism—embodied by objections to that "too foreign" aspect noted by Fu—continued to plague the most popular soy food, tofu, in the United States, with a long-running controversy about it containing estrogen and thus having "feminizing" properties—mirroring a common racist belief that Asian men were effeminate. This persists, with right-wing trolls on the internet using "soy boy" as an epithet toward liberals to suggest they're not manly enough.[10]

That original association of soy with poverty and deprivation never went away, though. In Cuba's "Special Period" after the collapse of the Soviet Union, upon which Cuba had relied for most of its trade, soy dairies sprung up to ensure an adequate protein supply.[11] In Romania, during times of economic strife, cookbooks provided recipes for soy salami and sausage to be served in place of beef or pork.[12]

And finally, soy's association in the US with the natural foods movement of the '70s has always done as much harm as good.

Motivated and energized by the anti–Vietnam War movement, food and bakery cooperatives began to spring up around the country, communes like The Farm in Tennessee became established and put out cookbooks, and the influence of *Diet for a Small Planet* and cookbooks like Anna Thomas's *The Vegetarian Epicure* and Mollie Katzen's *Moosewood Cookbook* created a real groundswell for a new way of thinking about food and relationships to the land. Organic farming and a rejection of industrial agriculture were becoming part of a bigger conversation, at least in certain circles.

What hurt the movement as well as the lasting reputation of tofu, tempeh, and seitan was the reality that the food wasn't always that good. Looking at the recipes now, one sees that the choice to eat like this would have to be compelled by a political or spiritual conviction rather than a desire to enjoy food. As Katzen herself told Epicurious in 2013, upon the release of her book *The Heart of the Plate: Vegetarian Recipes for a New Generation*, "Vegetarian then was, in a way, replacing the proverbial hunk of meat in the center of the American dinner plate with a hunk of something else. My early recipes came out in squares—the kugel, casserole, lasagna—so the main dish was replaced and the sides were the same: a side of vegetables, a side of salad."[13]

That lack of balance with acid and heat, along with a big focus on dairy at that time, means that those recipes from the '70s have a nostalgia factor but aren't in line with how people cook now. Olive oil, fresh herbs, more garlic, and homemade pickles, Katzen says, have changed her cooking. It was in the 1980s that olive oil really burst onto the scene in the US, gradually moving from the specialty store to the neighborhood grocer, influenced by health concerns around butter. There was more afoot, though, than just new reports on fat and the ongoing influence of "food establishment" members (as writer Nora Ephron called them in 1968) such as Julia Child and James Beard.[14]

It was also about the growing visibility of cooks and cuisines from non-European cultures where plant protein, vegetables, and grains had always taken on a more central role—whether out of poverty, a relationship to the dominant spiritual tradition, or a cultural understanding of sustainable eating before that became a buzzword, a problem to be solved by the intervention of corporate interests that could sell plant-based products. Books like *Chinese Vegetarian Cooking* by Florence Lin in 1976, *World-of-the-East Vegetarian Cooking* by Madhur Jaffrey in 1981, and *Classic Indian Vegetarian and Grain Cooking* by Julie Sahni in 1985 all aided in normalizing and expanding the narrow American perspective on vegetarian foods where meat had to be replaced with a heavy, hearty brick of dairy and egg.

In the tradition of Lappé and Shurtleff acting as stewards of eating for the planet in the US and translating meatless recipes to the white mainstream, Deborah Madison became the new face of vegetarian food, having come to her fame as the chef at Greens, a San Francisco farm-to-table restaurant associated with the Tassajara Zen Center, which opened in 1979.

Of Greens, the *New York Times* wrote in 2007, "It is the restaurant that brought vegetarian food out from sprout-infested health food stores and established it as a cuisine in America."[15] This is a common refrain from journalists who want to quickly say something about vegetarian food, and it leaves out the rich history of plant-centered diets common around the world. What the journalists mean here, really, is that it was through popular cookbooks like *The Greens Cookbook* and *Vegetarian Cooking for Everyone* that Greens (and, by extension, Deborah Madison) made vegetarian food that was simply *good food*— fresh and vegetable-focused, while still recognizably in the American, countercultural natural foods tradition.

As food writer and former editor-in-chief of *Gourmet* magazine Ruth Reichl remembered in 2021, "The sophisticated vegetarian menu [at Greens] was truly revolutionary for its time when most vegetarian restaurants were serving a high-minded version of sludge."[16] Joyce Goldstein, a chef and writer who chronicled the concept of "California food" in *Inside the California Food Revolution*, similarly writes: "At most of these places the food was earnest and well-meaning but rather heavy, combining grains and legumes to make complete proteins, garnished with nuts and seeds and accompanied by heaps of steamed vegetables sauced with tahini and tamari. Greens Restaurant, which opened in 1979, departed from the brown rice-and-veggies model by serving elegant vegetarian food in a beautiful setting on the San Francisco Bay."[17]

There are just a few tofu recipes in Madison's 1987 *Greens Cookbook*, demonstrating a move in the '80s away from the protein-obsessed version of vegetarian food that had been sold to people in the '70s. But to convince people to eat vegetables, the vegetables have to be really good, and that's what she had going for her in California, which is still a bastion of organic farming and was at the root of so much of the natural foods movement not just because of the concentration of hippies in San Francisco, but because of the quality of the produce itself. (As Eric Asimov wrote in the *New York Times* in 2001, "Even if many Americans are feeling new enthusiasm about vegetables, their attitude toward vegetarians is another matter," which is likely why neither Madison, Katzen, nor Lappé has ever identified herself as such—and has had success getting omnivores to eat their greens.)[18]

Madison would go on to write a book called *This Can't Be Tofu!* in 2000—after having big success with *Vegetarian Cooking for Everyone*—showing how tofu could be used in a versatile way to make traditional dishes and even vegan mayo.

Still, her approach to vegetarian cooking remained always "vegetable first," and that is broadly how vegetarian and vegan cooks, as well as omnivorous chefs playing with vegetables, have found success in the US. Charlie Trotter, the late fine-dining chef of his eponymous restaurant in Chicago, showed that vegetables could be compelling and made into precious dishes, such as rings of grain topped with braised mushroom, in his book *Charlie Trotter's Vegetables*, which came out in 1995. As vegan fine dining (or finer dining, at least) began to emerge, it was generally less protein-focused, too. Tal Ronnen, another California chef, in 2009's *The Conscious Cook*, wrote, "Tofu may have gained a reputation as a cliché of vegetarian food" as a way of saying it still has relevance, but he does use it rather judiciously in his recipes.

It's interesting that while the "protein question" continues to be a constant refrain in the world of plant-heavy eating, from omnivores to vegetarians and vegans, the food—as a cuisine, with guiding principles and techniques—has only ever been taken seriously when protein isn't the star on the plate. There is something about the meat-reared American palate that has historically been averse to considering anything that isn't animal-derived a "real" protein, and when eating vegetarian or vegan food, prefers to consume just vegetables—perhaps an extension of the idea that the impetus to forgo meat must come from a focus on health and purity.

I'm someone who loves vegetable-forward vegetarian and vegan food, too, and so I'm guilty of perpetuating the "weirdness" factor when I encounter a heaping plate of plant protein. My favorite restaurants and cookbooks are the ones where, as at the no-longer-open Nix, I might be served a whole beet in a bun—a play on the concept of the veggie burger. At Dirt Candy, I thrill to eat mushroom mousse and tomato tarts and fried rings of squash. I keep tofu, tempeh, and seitan to their initial cultural contexts. But I wonder whether this does a disservice to how they're perceived. Would we need an Impossible Burger if Americans who didn't grow up with it saw tofu as a regular part of their weekly dinner rotation?

I can't help but think that this has done a disservice to the broad approachability and accessibility of meatless cuisine. People like to have "a protein" because it's a way to feel full, yes, and because it helps organize a plate. Tofu, especially, is a cheap and healthy way to create a "main course" that is recognizable as such and that fills up the eater. One block of extra firm tofu can usually be found for under $5 and will feed four people, at least. Instead of making memes mocking the omnivores who ask, "Where do you get your protein?" it's a good moment to remember that kale is expensive, beans take a lot of time and know-how to prepare, and—as Shurtleff, Aoyagi, and The Farm commune told us—the replacements for hunks of meat were developed a couple of thousand years ago in China and Indonesia.

There has been a recent resurgence of interest in tofu and other traditional plant proteins. Soy saw a new increase in consumption when the COVID-19 pandemic began to cause lockdowns and various food shortages (or the threat of food shortages) in the US. Sales of tofu went through the roof.[19] Not only were stories about the horrors of meat-processing workers being forced to work in close quarters throughout this time unavoidable, but many folks with more time to cook yet wanting to go to the grocery store less to minimize exposure started to stock up on tofu. Its availability and comparatively long shelf-life, along with the newly plant-curious using this moment to reassess their relationship to meat in light of its intersection with other social concerns around climate and labor, made tofu a newly appealing option. What also could have helped change tofu's reputation has been the proliferation of more regional Chinese restaurants, which have shown increasing numbers of people there are many rich and flavorful ways to enjoy this plant protein.

It's telling that vegan and vegetarian restaurants on their own weren't able to usher in this kind of change; traditional preparations or innovative approaches by chefs who grew up with these ingredients not as meat replacements but ingredients in their own right have been the key to opening people's eyes in the US to what is possible with a plant-driven diet. But vegan and vegetarian restaurants themselves have been key in revealing how much has changed in the attitudes of people who have given up meat, and it's our relationship to protein that has always been defining. The shift in New York City alone tells a story.

Of course, no one wants to hear a bridge-and-tunnel kid bemoan the inevitable changes to New York City, and they especially don't want to hear it from a vegetarian one. But the developments in the preparation of vegetables, in non-vegetarian and veg restaurants, have reconfigured the entire vegan cuisine order. Where would I go now for a Peanut Butter Bomb shipped in from Vegan Treats in Pennsylvania to follow up a bean-based chili and cornbread, as I did at Teany before going to see a band at Bowery Ballroom in the mid-'00s?

(Nowhere, but I could have something much tastier at Superiority Burger.) Could I get a non-dairy banana split after getting my nose pierced on Second Avenue? (Yes, but today I'd get it at the sleek Van Leeuwen chain.)

From fast food to ice cream to health food institutions, it seems as though an entire cultural shift has taken place, and it's not just high rent that's to blame (though that never helps). The cause, counterintuitively, seems to be the increasing popularity of vegetables and faux-meat fast-food burger facsimiles. An entire era of vegan food in the city, wiped out by its own relevance.

The list of dead restaurants runs long, and someone's favorite is always bound to be left off. But to name the major players, the ones who received mainstream food blog obituaries: Kate's Joint, the vegetarian diner on the corner of Avenue B and East Fourth Street, shut down in 2012, then Williamsburg's Foodswings followed in 2014, and raw joint Pure Food and Wine and Moby-owned Teany closed up in 2015. Blythe Ann's ice cream shop, the second incarnation of Lula's Sweet Apothecary, was cleared out in 2016. In 2017, it was Angelica Kitchen's turn, serving its final macrobiotic sushi roll and carob tart. At the end of 2019, when Candle 79 blew out its lights and the Jivamuktea Café shuttered, it seemed as though all the vegan restaurants that defined New York's meatless dining scene had said goodbye, yet still there were more to go: at the end of March, food truck and The Pennsy stall Cinnamon Snail served its last raspberry blackout doughnut and maple mustard tempeh sandwich.

Angelica Kitchen had been around since 1976; the others had shorter but no less influential runs. Foodswings opened in 2003, serving tofu buffalo wings, seitan gyros, and other staples that were heavy on the classic vegan proteins. That's the kind of food that its first owner, Freedom Tripodi, a Bronx native who gave up animal products as a teenager, missed. He was frustrated with what was available at the time, spots that focused mainly on health food, macrobiotics, and more dainty presentations rather than analogues of what omnivores were accustomed to eating at cheap prices.

What he sees now at current vegan restaurants in New York is, again, a lack of focus on proteins, which to him is a detriment. But the ethos of Foodswings remains available at Champs Diner in Bushwick, which opened in 2010 and focuses on seitan and processed cheese products. The owners added the Instagram-ready Hartbreakers in 2018, noting the shifting cultural tone toward an aesthetic with broader appeal to those outside vegan and vegetarian in-groups; it has a decidedly more updated vibe complete with neon signage, and everything but the bread and sliced cheese is made in-house. The Impossible and Beyond Burgers make headlines for their fast-food and retail success, so now omnivores can get something meat-like just about anywhere, but the signature veggie burger made of beans and grains continues to be the vegan preference. Tripodi's Foodswings menu approach feels nostalgic, as much a product of its time as Angelica's tempeh rolls or Candle 79's gingered brown rice or Pure Food and Wine's raw lasagna. These days in vegan cuisine, neither health nor indulgence reign, but rather some medium between the two, focused on quality sourcing and an inclusive dietary approach, such as a soy-free kitchen where the tofu is made with chickpea flour, Burmese style.

Chef Amanda Cohen, who's been running Dirt Candy since 2008 and opened the more casual Lekka Burger in 2020, could be considered responsible for the shift toward vegetables being taken more seriously at both omnivorous and vegan restaurants. She graduated from the Natural Gourmet Institute in the late '90s, eventually working at Teany, opening the kitchen of Pure Food and Wine, and going on to Heirloom, a vegetarian and raw restaurant where every dish was made three ways (vegan, vegetarian, and raw).

"I wanted to open my own restaurant because, while I hadn't worked at every restaurant in the city, they were all on the same level," she says. Kitchens she had wanted to work in, like Kate's Joint and Chinese vegetarian places, didn't give her any opportunities. "I knew enough about the kitchens at the time that I didn't really feel like a lot of the vegetarian kitchens were putting out the most exciting food.

I thought there was a whole other world out there. And I worked in the kitchen in the city for a number of years and I could work under some great chefs and some really crappy chefs, but I definitely started to develop my own style," she says.

At that point, she'd been cooking professionally for fifteen years but saw no innovation in vegetarian cooking, while traditional restaurants were changing so much. The only reason, in her view, for these places getting new customers was that there was turnover in people trying out vegetarian or vegan diets; it wasn't a matter of omnivores coming in because they were excited about the food. That isn't the foundation of a sustainable business model, and Cohen would know: Dirt Candy has been open and successful since 2008, and now Lekka Burger serves globally inspired veggie burgers with a base recipe derived from the Ming Dynasty and onion rings, crinkle-cut fries, and oat milk shakes.

If you dig a bit further, though, Cohen in particular has been significant not just for her food and hospitality ethos (living wage and health care for employees, among other benefits) but because she runs an explicitly vegetarian restaurant in a chef's manner. This is a marriage of a chef's technique, as she learned at the Natural Gourmet Institute, and a fun and fantastical approach to vegetables that is decidedly secular—as in, not influenced by spirituality, wellness, or a hippie perspective.[20] Therein lies her success, which has allowed a similar approach to proliferate: Superiority Burger, while decidedly not fine dining, is unapologetically vegetarian while wildly delicious. Vedge, in Philadelphia, is a vegan restaurant that is fine dining without proselytizing. Moto Foto, also in Philly, was a vegan pop-up that smoked mushrooms and fried baby artichokes to serve with kumquat aioli.

These places aren't Charlie Trotter or Grant Achatz of Alinea doing a vegetarian or vegan tasting menu on the side. They are vegetables, grains, and legumes—as well as "fatty ass nuts," to use Moto Foto's vernacular—as perpetual stars, without pretension and without proselytizing. When guests have asked Cohen about protein, she's asked them what they ate for lunch that day, reminding folks that there is protein in every plant-based food and that it's not the only reason to eat (also, most people in the US get too much protein as it is).

As plant-based and vegan dining has gone mainstream, though, some sense of the food as countercultural, alternative, and radical has also been lost—which is a good thing when it comes to getting people to eat more plants, but feels like the erasure of how deeply rooted this kind of eating has long been in an approach to life that rejects not just the Standard American Diet of meat and potatoes but the Standard American Perspective that privileges individualism over community. That was the ethos that intrigued me, the bridge-and-tunnel kid, and got me excited to eat bean-based chili. It's what keeps me reading about The Farm and watching documentaries on food cooperatives. Tripodi of Foodswings notes that when they opened, they weren't focused just on promoting animal rights, but on making sure they were part of the community in Williamsburg as it rapidly gentrified. Jivamuktea didn't let its patrons forget that their vegan sandwich was part of curbing the suffering of all beings.

This is a simplification, of course. The same racial and economic forces that have determined how people eat have changed quite a bit since the '70s; there is much more openness to flavors from around the world, making the nuances of how various plant proteins are understood in society seem not all that significant. Yet there has been a subtle shift in availability and understanding. The Target store by my mom's house on Long Island now has a small section in the refrigerated food that is stocked with marinated Hodo Soy tofu, Lightlife tempeh, Uptons Naturals seitan, and Field Roast's sausages, which have wheat gluten as a major ingredient. (The way that we talk about the success of "plant-based food" through its availability as processed food products, though, will be discussed later in the book.) Making these plant proteins accessible means making a diet less dependent on meat seem much more doable, and this is the legacy of various cooks, cookbook authors, and historians but also the folks who started tofu companies way back in 1878, who kept cooking seitan even when it wasn't that cool, and folks, like Barry Schwartz, who continue to ask passersby on the street to try tempeh.

The New American plant-based cuisine is a product of all these approaches, from the hippie commune to the punk café to the fine-dining restaurant. These alternative proteins and vegetable-forward cooking styles have stood the test of time by becoming more popular, more accessible, and more delicious. Though meat still reigns in the United States, there is a lot more openness and understanding of why it's important to push animal protein into a smaller section of one's plate and daily diet, and there are more recipes and ingredients available to help the average person do that, whether they're shopping at a neighborhood food co-op or a big-box store.

As I write this in 2022, there are still complaints about the "preachy vegan" despite fast-food appeals to meatless diets. That cliché may have been borne out of these vegan restaurants of yore, now gone, replaced by vegetable-forward dining and Instagram-friendly new spaces. What we've gained in better seasoned food, less reliance on brown rice, and pleas for animal rights, we've lost in the feeling of doing something against the grain—even if that grain is now heirloom farro. I'll happily eat my non-dairy Van Leeuwen banana split in the East Village of today, but I'll be thinking of the not-so-distant past, when I would have to go to Lula's Sweet Apothecary's hole-in-the-wall spot—when even though vegetables were everywhere, finding vegan food felt like a miracle. When it felt cool, part of the lineage of all these folks who saw a way forward that could keep the human population from suffering hunger and the effects of global warming. Now, plant-based eating is often understood as a luxury good and a list of brand-name products rather than ingredients. How did it go from the hippie communes to becoming not just a cuisine, but a mark of decadence?

4. TOWARD A POLITICAL PALATE

E dward Espe Brown, in his 1970 *Tassajara Bread Book*, recommends Erewhon as a source for corn germ oil that is high in essential fatty acids and antioxidants. Today, Erewhon—which began as a natural foods distributor in 1966—is known as a "luxury" grocery store catering to various alternative diets. There is a CEO, and a private equity firm has become a "substantial" minority stakeholder. "How Erewhon Became L.A.'s Hottest Hangout," read a 2021 *New York Times* headline.[1] Hippies started something, and now their counterculture moment has become a rich person's way to eat. Or at least it's perceived that way.

From Erewhon, to Tassajara Zen Center and The Farm commune, to *Diet for a Small Planet*, to *The Vegetarian Epicure*, there was clear evidence of a counterculture that rejected industrial agriculture, especially large-scale, intensive animal agriculture, and the ways of eating associated with it, in the late 1960s into the 1970s. The people creating this counterculture were questioning whether a style of eating based on convenience and overuse of resources to the detriment of not just animal welfare but global hunger (as Lappé chronicled) would adversely affect personal health and the future of the planet. Lappé famously called the American diet experimental, noting that neither the centrality of meat nor the liberal use of pesticides had any basis in traditional human diets.

And so, there was an attempt to create a New American Cuisine with a plant-centered ethos, one that could sustain people and planet. Few were more committed to the cause than the three hundred folks who followed Stephen Gaskin from California to Summertown, Tennessee, where they established an intentional community they called The Farm in 1970.

Gaskin had been teaching English at San Francisco State when he was given a Monday night slot that became known simply as "Monday Night Class," where Gaskin would expound upon spiritual and philosophical matters. He also allowed others to speak, in a kind of forum setting. It went from a church to a theater, where five hundred to a thousand people were estimated to be in attendance on any given week. This led to invitations to speak at churches and universities around the country, his community traveling in a caravan of fifty buses. Upon their return, they found San Francisco had changed, and cited the use of hard drugs as reason to leave. The buses once again made their way out of California, this time heading to Tennessee, where they'd eventually buy a thousand acres of land at $70 per acre.

What set The Farm apart from the stereotypical idea of a hippie commune—and perhaps why the commune still functions today—was Gaskin's insistence on practical responsibilities that was part of his ethos and was found in dictums such as, "If you're sleeping together, you're engaged; if you're pregnant, you're married. No one walks away from a baby," and "Work is the material plane expression of love," which was his interpretation of Buddhism's right livelihood principle. To make their way of life more than a fad, they had to take their very survival seriously. That included farming and cooking. (As well as midwifery: Ina May Gaskin, Stephen's wife, has been one of the most influential midwives on the planet.)

It's easy to focus on the "strangeness" of a communal lifestyle and the cult-like figure cut by someone like Gaskin, but the reality is that their methods of farming and cooking weren't born of a fad but out of a real understanding of how to feed a lot of people cheaply while tending to the soil and without taking life through animal husbandry. While *The Farm Vegetarian Cookbook*, written by Louise Hagler and published in 1975, painted a picture of abundance, with black-and-white photos of smiling hippies cooking and pouring soft-serve "ice bean" made of soy milk into traditional ice cream shop cups, some former members painted a dire picture of communal deprivation when the number of people living at the commune swelled to over 1,200 in the late '70s and early '80s. In a 1985 interview with *Whole Earth Review*, one of them remembered: "The last year we were at the Farm somebody gave a bunch of money to buy the Farm a nice meal for Christmas day. So we bought noodles and oranges. While we're eating noodles, Rose, our daughter, said, 'I wish we could have noodles sometime besides just for Christmas.' And I thought, my God, that's really pretty bad."[2]

That tracks with other accounts of commune life. Reporters would often visit hippies looking for sex parties, but food was always the biggest topic of discussion and concern. As Stephanie Hartman wrote in "The Political Palate: Reading Commune Cookbooks," the mood at dinner told you everything about the level of communal spirit in the group: "A good dinner represented communal life at its best," she wrote. "After working together, everyone got to reap the rewards."[3] The feeling of scarcity at dinner and the accounts of kids stealing oranges because they were hungry was one reason The Farm changed dramatically in the early '80s.

In 1983, the people of The Farm came together and voted to end the collective to become a cooperative in which everyone would work and pay dues. The number of members then decreased to a more manageable 250, where it has more or less stayed until this day. They've formed businesses on the land that help sustain its livelihood, including a publishing arm, midwifery center, and Tempeh Lab (which produces the cultures necessary to the formation of tempeh), proving that this model of living can work when a balance is achieved and members of the collective have attained a vision not so dependent on one individual. Food continues to be grown and processed on The Farm's premises, including beans, okra, and other vegetables.

Perhaps the most influential aspect of The Farm has been its vegan culinary vision, first articulated in *The Farm Vegetarian Cookbook* and refined in many releases on vegetarian and vegan food through its book publishing company. While Shurtleff and Aoyagi have been credited with popularizing tofu, miso, and tempeh in the US, the expertise required to make it had already been deeply documented at The Farm, and it was The Farm that tipped Shurtleff off to tempeh's very existence.

Commune member Alexander Lyon, who had a PhD in biochemistry from the California Institute of Technology, dove into the potential of the soybean while visiting his family in New York for Christmas in 1971. He was especially interested in creating a vegan product that could wean babies, which was how he found soy milk, and by extension, also tempeh and miso. He returned to The Farm and started its Soy Dairy, where experimentations led to cheese and yogurt-like soy products, and in 1972 the two-page manual titled "Tempeh Instructions." As the Soy Dairy continued to evolve, another member, Laurie Sythe Praskin, figured out how to scale tofu production so that it could be more regularly available to eat.

The beauty of The Farm's cookbooks is in their simplicity. The instructions for making tofu and tempeh are laid out over the course of a few pages. Though they were a spiritual group of folks, they were nondenominational, part of the break with the vegetarian past represented by Lappé's *Diet for a Small Planet*: their recipes were accessible and based on foods people were accustomed to eating, with some "one-world" nods to non-Western cuisines. An updated edition of one of the cookbooks features "dahl," on a page with a paisley illustration. There's tofu grilled cheese, in which tofu is crumbled with "melty nutritional yeast 'cheese,'" placed between slices of bread, and grilled in margarine. Soysage is made with the pulp left over from making soy milk, combined with whole wheat flour, wheat germ, oil, and spices. It's not until deep in the book that vegetables stand alone, in a brief salad chapter, but broccoli stir-fry and cabbage carrot casserole provide heartier fare while not being completely soy-based.

It's easy to laugh at the very concept of commune cooking, but the studied nature of the work at The Farm means there are many ideas here that foreshadow the future of vegan cooking, which would only become popularized in the late 2000s with a boom of mainstream cookbooks that included no animal products whatsoever. Feeding so many people and using what was available, while also spending so much time in the kitchen, yielded some lasting food science. The fingerprints of these recipes would come to be all over the punk and anarchist vegan cookzines of the '80s and '90s, then trickle up to more professional chefs who had roots in that subculture. What The Farm's recipe writers call "bean juice"—the liquid left in the pot from cooking soybeans—is a precursor to the now widespread use of aquafaba, the gooey liquid in a can of chickpeas that can whip up like egg whites, bind baked goods, and provide a white froth on shaken cocktails like a whiskey sour.

Desserts are the strongest point in the book, with the recipe writers clearly more enthusiastic about white cake and fluffy icing than millet and peas. The contrast is interesting: there are few headnotes in the book, and the recipes really stand on their own, with some ingredients only given in the course of the directions. Savory recipes are workhorse recipes, clearly meant for providing nutrition and feeding a large group. The desserts are plentiful and generally redolent of Americana—sweet potato pie, white cake, brownies, gingerbread, pancakes, Danish, apple cobbler, and oatmeal cookies. I could be projecting my own subjective preference for sweets, but while the savory recipes look forward toward a soy foods future that is more inclusive of global cuisines, the desserts are tinged with nostalgia for lives that were left behind—lives where more traditional middle-class mothers made traditional desserts for their families.

One of the more compelling concepts that would go on to be refined over the next few decades is the use of tofu for creamy pies. Chocolate tofu cream pie comes with the note, "This is a rich one," and in tofu cheesecake, all that's used to give a cream cheese tang is lemon juice; this is a simplicity of thought that I adore, one that recognizes that while vegan baked goods might not necessarily be exactly like their traditional counterparts, there's still joy in replicating familiar textures and flavors. They are created anew, with political consciousness, while retaining the comfort of the known.

These are still common ways of making vegan cream pies and cheesecakes, which are made in a blender. Silken tofu is now more commonly used as an egg replacement than firm tofu because of its smoother mouthfeel. (It was developed in Japan during World War II, when the natural *nigari*, or magnesium chloride, used to curdle soy milk in production was being used in military plane construction, leaving tofu-makers with calcium sulfate and thus changing the texture.)

The recipes that become joke fodder for people wanting to mock vegan commune cooking are the ones that focus on nutritional yeast as a cheese replacement or the suggestion of blending oil (the type of oil goes unspecified) with soy milk and spices to create "soy nog" at holiday time. These show commitment to the cause, but they won't convert anyone.

Conversion wasn't really the point of a cookbook like this, though; it was a way of sharing information and intelligence that had been gathered from experience, and some of that has stood the test of time. Many communes were explicitly *not* vegetarian or vegan, and while they may have experimented with "soy balls" and other foods, they would also unapologetically hunt and eat wild animals or whatever was available. There has never been one "counterculture cuisine," though vegetarian ideas have been deeply tied to it because of associations with Tassajara Zen Center and *Diet for a Small Planet*.

One must admit that, while the vegetarian movement has been somewhat influential, most people then and now have been reluctant to label themselves or their food vegetarian—and for perhaps good reason, because while people have come around to new vegetables, the percentage of people in the US who identify as vegan or vegetarian has stayed pretty stagnant over time. Tiny victories have been blown up into major wins. Yes, there is tofu at Target—but where's the evidence that people are really thinking differently about how they live and how food fits in as a very significant part of that lifestyle, which was a real consideration of the counterculture food movement? Organic foods are so prevalent that they have a lobby in Washington, DC, and conventional agribusiness sells organics side by side with industrially manufactured products. It's not much different from corporate meat companies making profits on ultra-processed meat alternatives while still slaughtering animals. What hippies left behind in terms of information on new and alternative food is invaluable—but their legacy would be better served by those with a stronger ethos than simply peace and love.

There are a few theories for why this way of life more or less faded into obscurity in the early '80s, one of which is that, clearly, staying apolitical—by which I mean, not working for policy change that would make life better for everyone and not just those who shed their earthly material belongings—made communes look like a curiosity, a relic. Writer Jonathan Kauffman, author of *Hippie Food*, hypothesizes that the communes began to dissolve when people of that generation were turning thirty and looking for a more stable way of life. The forces that had spurred the counterculture, from the 1962 release of Rachel Carson's environmentalist tract *Silent Spring*, to civil rights and Vietnam War activism, to *Diet for a Small Planet*, lost their luster after so many years spent subsisting on soybeans—right down to soy coffee. There was also the reality that this moment had been quite white, and when one's body is no longer subject to overtly coercive state power—when the military draft is ended—there is a real pull toward a return to mainstream, middle-class life. For those whose bodies are always already political, whether because of race, gender, sexuality, class, or an intersection of these, it is not so easy nor attractive to simply dip back into the culture from the counterculture or other movements.

Gretchen Lemke-Santangelo, a history professor at St. Mary's College of California, documented the demographics of the counterculture in her 2009 book *Daughters of Aquarius: Women of the Sixties*

Counterculture.[4] The hippies were rather evenly divided by gender, but in terms of race, she writes that fewer than 3 percent were nonwhite. Giving up stability held little appeal for those whose lives were challenged already, who didn't have a cushion to fall back on when times got tough and didn't find anything appealing about the "leisure" of the hippie class. As well, white hippie women often fetishized Black and Indigenous men, thinking them as keyholders to a deeper consciousness based wholly in stereotypes, and many women of color didn't see the appeal of free love and the sexual revolution when they had already spent centuries being seen only for their bodies. Men and women of color already had groups working in their political and cultural interest, while much of the counterculture seemed to be composed of lazy, privileged white kids despite their purported political agenda. This had repercussions for just how much impact the broader counterculture could have and how we assess it: it's fun to laugh at the hippies or to dip into their cookbooks for a glimpse at how they lived; it's not as fun to think about how this way of living was replicating oppressions and exclusions that it purported to be wholly against. This had caused splits and factions among the counterculture, between those more interested in a lifestyle change and the New Left, among others, seeking a more politically engaged way of life.

The Farm's most influential contribution in the last thirty years has been that of member Albert Bates, who wrote the book *Climate in Crisis* in 1990 with a foreword from then senator Al Gore. Though Stephen Gaskin died in 2014, the dream lives on at a smaller scale, and his influence has been an undeniable force in vegan cooking ever since—regardless of the dominant subculture.

This tension between a hippie perspective and a more stringent radical politics—one that recognizes the very body that is on the line—has been one that has allowed food to be perceived as separate from its origins, as a style of cooking, eating, and resistance to corporate power. We know now that whole wheat bread on its own doesn't have any political meaning, yet it does have power as a foundation for political consciousness. This difference in perspective had been a point of antagonism in the late '60s and early '70s between the New Left and the hippies—the political versus the personal—and it would continue to be a point of contention, but the feminist movement would give better shape to concrete ways of achieving a truly egalitarian world. Indeed, it marked the moment when the personal was fully recognized as political. When an ecofeminist-vegetarian movement took root, the political meaning of food would not be erased.

The Political Palate came out in 1980, a decade after Edward Espe Brown's *Tassajara Bread Book* and—continuing in the style of the counterculture book—includes asides and poems and manifestos along with recipes, a zine-like way of collaging influences and ensuring that readers could continue in their education on various subjects like the poetry of Adrienne Rich and the thinking of Audre Lorde. But there's a clear edge in this text, one that could alienate a more genteel hippie who came up in the natural foods heyday.

The book was a product of the Bloodroot Collective, which opened its Bloodroot Restaurant and Feminist Bookstore in Bridgeport, Connecticut, in 1977. Today, it's still open and operating, though no longer a collective in function; it's run by Selma Miriam and Noel Furie, who have been there since the outset. Miriam had been attending women's groups for ages; she took money she'd saved from her landscape design business to start her own women's center. A bookstore seemed an ideal model, but she loved cooking and wanted to add a restaurant. To be a feminist at this time and not wholly reject the domestic was certainly more in line with the hippies than the New Left, and at Bloodroot—which was explicitly for women—this joy in domestic tasks took on a new character.

"My friends said it should be vegetarian if it was going to be feminist, so I'd make vegetarian food and then go home and cook chicken," Miriam told me in an interview on a quiet Saturday afternoon between lunch and dinner service in 2015.[5] Eventually, she became vegetarian herself.

The connection between vegetarianism and feminism has its roots in the concept of ecofeminism, a term coined in 1974 by the French writer Françoise d'Eaubonne in her book *Le féminisme ou la mort*. In the text, she draws connections between women's subjugation under patriarchy and the destruction of nature; one way to extend this concept is into vegetarianism, wherein the oppression of women in society is analogous to the use of animals for livestock and the production of goods.

This theory has undergone rigorous critique over the years for taking an essentialist perspective on women and nature, as well as for not being intersectional in terms of race, class, and gender identity. These critiques have had merit, though often were used specifically against vegetarian ecofeminists in support of the consumption of animals. In the time since "ecofeminism" peaked in usage in the '80s and '90s, there has been a reclamation of the term, with a broader application that accounts for racial, gender, and food sovereignty in the Global South as well as myriad differences in experience, while still accounting for the necessity of feminist critique when it comes to the human relationship with nature.[6]

Miriam and Furie are explicitly ecofeminist in their texts and worldview, which, Alex Ketchum writes in her dissertation "Serving Up Revolution: Feminist Restaurants, Cafés, and Coffeehouses in the United States and Canada from 1972 to 1989," creates a "feminist food":

> The Bloodroot Collective explicitly put ecofeminism at the fore-
> front of its vision for the restaurant. In the collective's third cook-
> book, *The Perennial Palate*, the members stated, "Eating meat is
> wrong for its cruelty to creatures who can feel and experience pain,
> and wrong because it contributes to worldwide starvation, mostly
> of women and children." In no way was being vegetarian an acci-
> dent or by-product of another cultural influence. The Bloodroot
> Collective members repeatedly insisted that their vegetarianism
> was integral to their feminism and that the food they served was
> feminist itself.[7]

Their focus on communal cooking, learning, and service has easily lent itself to adaptations to other concerns, and over time the food they serve has become more local, seasonal, and vegan, as the environmental impact of dairy has become more clear and urgent. The customers have also simply demanded it.

Without formal culinary training, Miriam wanted to create recipes that would be easily made by all who worked there. Bloodroot isn't run in the hierarchical manner of a formal restaurant—there is no one who goes by the title of chef—and so everyone who runs food, takes orders, and helps in the kitchen also works the stove. Miriam's liberal with giving out recipes, having published five cookbooks since 1980, so they're all easily made by home cooks as well. The kitchen itself is a marriage of the professional and domestic, with dishes stacked high on shelves and spices tucked into a corner. Customers place their order at the desk, pick up their food when it's ready, and bring their check to the kitchen counter when their meal is over. Then they clear their own table.

The restaurant's cuisine and the collective nature of how the operation is run are meant to evoke comfort, to promote consciousness and community. Stepping into Bloodroot means stepping into a home, quite literally. It is a renovated residential house on a quiet block, with a backyard that overlooks Long Island Sound. The chairs and tables in the big, open dining room are mismatched, framed pictures of women line the walls, and blankets bought on travels are draped over the ceiling beams to soften the echo in the room as well as its look. In a place where you bus your own tables, such homey comfort is necessary to keep customers coming back. It also, the co-owners say, keeps away those who feel more entitled.

Bloodroot is the last restaurant of its kind, according to Ketchum, a former Bloodroot regular who started the Feminist Restaurant Project as part of her doctoral research. More than forty years after it opened, during a tiny boom of second-wave feminist bookstores and restaurants, it's surviving, according to Miriam, for three reasons:

"We work in a very pretty place; it's not a busy spot, but we're needed. We also really like cooking. And also, the way we're structured," she told me in an interview.

Customers regularly travel to the restaurant. "Those women came from Albany," Miriam said, gesturing to a full table. "When they don't come, we worry about them." It's a place not just to eat, but to immerse yourself in the kind of political space that's difficult to find nowadays. Above the counter, a sign says, "Because all women are victims of Fat Oppression and out of respect for women of size, we would appreciate your refraining from agonizing aloud over the calorie count in our food."

This unabashed demand upon customers to respect the feminist politics of the space while within it has been integral to the restaurant's success and longevity as not just a business but a continued creator of feminist consciousness.

In keeping with their sign against calorie-count discussion, Bloodroot, in its food, has always fought against the health food ideology that plagues the reputation of vegetarian cooking. Miriam recently gave a talk at a local library in which she went through all the diet fads that have come and gone since the restaurant's opening. Its timeless focus on global home cooking and whole foods has kept it relevant, whether people were avoiding fat, carbs, or gluten. It also strives to be an antidote to junk-based meatless eating. "American vegan food is ghastly," Miriam said.

What this comment refers to is the image of the American vegan who cares only whether or not there are animal products in their food, not whether the ingredients were sourced well, prepared with care, or have nutritional value. It's the vegan food of the Foodswings era, tofu buffalo wings dipped in a sauce based on Vegenaise. A theorist of ecofeminism, Greta Gaard, has suggested that not only is vegetarianism a tenet of the ecofeminist framework, but so is sustainable agricultural practice, and that idea is expressed in Bloodroot's practice.

On the summer Saturday when I visited in 2015, the menu was almost completely vegan, showing the Bloodroot approach to cutting out dairy and egg. Highly recommended was the jerk seitan and tofu, a recipe brought in by a woman from Jamaica named Carol who was cooking in the kitchen. The hunks of grilled seitan were incredibly spicy and juicy—the latter an adjective you can rarely apply to seitan. It was served with rice and beans and baked sweet potato, both of which serve to balance out the intensity of the jerk spices. It's recommended that you pair the dish with a sorrel-hibiscus juice that Carol also brought onto the menu, which is floral and sour, sweet and cooling.

Miriam showed me how she makes "the best" pie crust, which uses melted coconut oil and is based on a recipe for one made with lard that she'd read in the *Times*. It requires only a fork and a bowl, meaning it's achievable for anyone, but does require some finesse to get into the pie plate because it's extremely temperature sensitive. With the crust, she made a blueberry pie for that night's dessert menu, which also included raspberry mousse, chocolate pudding, a hot fudge sundae, and brown rice pudding. It's dessert as your mom would make it, a quaint reprieve from the splatters and spoon swooshing of most restaurant plating. This too harkens back to the reclamation of the domestic by feminists of the '70s, who were able to subvert what it meant for a woman to be in the kitchen, providing nourishment. At Bloodroot, to be a woman in the kitchen also meant to be working in community and, for Miriam and Furie, living independently.

Their cookbooks, too, are an anomaly, with political essays in the front that recommend the work of extremely controversial feminists. *The Second Seasonal Political Palate*, published in 1984, has a blurb from famed lesbian poet Adrienne Rich. If you can't stifle your colloquial tic of referring to everyone as "you guys" despite their writings on its insulting male-centeredness (I, a millennial from Long Island, could not when I visited), they politely ask to be referred to as "women." They have remained staunchly second wave in a world that's moved through its third, perhaps fourth waves.

When asked how they feel about the recent upswing in a brand of feminism that is more about personal choice than political revolution,

Miriam and Furie rolled their eyes. "We tread more carefully," Furie noted. They took down a poster against high heels that had been in the bathroom, and now don't feel as free to discuss fashion or beauty ideals as aspects of patriarchal oppression.

Despite keeping themselves away from TV and computers as much as possible, the outside world has affected their idyllic women's space, but not by much. It's probably the sole surviving feminist restaurant of its kind in the US because of the owners' steadfastness, as well as their openness to new foods and all who walk through their doors. They have a running list of all the countries customers have visited from, and themselves go on a trip every year. As Miriam says, "All of these things feed us back."

Though they wear their politics on their sleeves and in signage at the restaurant, they've also always taken the food seriously. In the introduction to *The Second Seasonal Political Palate*, they note that "earlier books" of vegetarian recipes "were often disappointing to us as serious vegetarian cooks." Miriam and Furie's recipes include miso gravy deepened by the flavor of Guinness stout; kombu used to bring out umami; shallot wine hollandaise; and frozen tofu in place of pork in the Caribbean soup *sancocho*. The recipes express a global palate, with Indian dishes like dahl and Mexican enchiladas, and a focus on using soy proteins in a Western context, recognizing the significance of these proteins to sustaining a vegetarian diet.

In 2007, they put out two lengthy volumes of their recipes titled *The Best of Bloodroot*. Volume 1 contains vegetarian recipes; Volume 2 is all vegan. These books maintain the strong feminist, vegetarian, and ecological position of their '80s books. To start the vegan edition, their coauthor (and influential vegan chef) Lagusta Yearwood writes about replacing dairy with coconut and the potential that lies therein, as well as the potential for a vision beyond one purely focused on animal rights: "When vegetarians and vegans limit politics to the realm of animal rights, we are doing ourselves a disservice. If Bloodroot has taught us anything in its almost three decades of existence, it is that feminism, progressive politics, animal rights, and environmentalism work best when they work together."

This is where Bloodroot's specific perspective and impressive longevity also stand apart from the work of those women who came out of the counterculture movement to become successful authors of vegetarian cookbooks, like Deborah Madison and Mollie Katzen, neither of whom has taken on the label of "vegetarian." Madison fully rejects it, writing an entire chapter in her memoir *An Onion in My Pocket* titled "My Vegetarian Problem." She eats meat brought over by rancher friends and talks about pitiful vegan versions of her dishes that readers have attempted. In an essay for *The Counter*, she writes: "I love vegetables, but eating them is not a salve. We can't escape from the fact of our eating; no matter what, we are killing living things so that we can live ourselves. If it's not an animal, it's a plant or something else. What matters more is that food tastes good and that it's sourced responsibly."[8]

That's all well and good, but it's also often going to be read as a capitulation: When the individual is the focus, who's forgotten? People for whom the only accessible meat is industrially produced, processed by poorly paid and overworked laborers. One doesn't have to be vegetarian, but there are concerns beyond one's personal values and one's own access to meat that is "sourced responsibly," and creating real accessibility to such meat would be part and parcel of ending industrial animal agriculture. Indeed, it would create a new world—culturally and economically—to see the American diet shift to less meat that has been ethically reared and slaughtered.

The ethos emerging from counterculture views regarding vegetarianism and responsible food sourcing splintered in two directions: one more commercial and the other more radical. Many more people have cooked from the recipes of Madison and Katzen, of course, though I find myself wishing that vegetarianism didn't have to be thrown out as a way of approaching the world. That nothing can be perfect doesn't mean that ethics shouldn't be part of a serious effort.

The depoliticization of this way of eating by those who were once its most visible advocates has been understandable yet disappointing, as it becomes more and more clear how necessary it will be for people in the US to move toward a plant-based diet.

There has forever been controversy about whether to eat meat or not in what Warren Belasco termed the "countercuisine" in his book *Appetite for Change: How the Counterculture Took on the Food Industry*. Vegetarian communes were more common on the West Coast, whereas on the East, people were more likely to eat meat because they found it economical. And yet others got into whole animal butchery and eating nose-to-tail—including drinking blood. The countercuisine had no official stance on meat (that would go against the whole idea, man) but the very idea that meat-eating needed to be thought through, all its angles considered, was a significant aspect of questioning the ideology of mainstream American eating. Even if popular vegetarian cookbook authors might not want to be so overtly connected to animal rights, there is still a deeply political and feminist strain to vegetarian and vegan thought that has been inextricable from vegetarian food as a cuisine. As Lagusta Yearwood put it, being against agribusiness and for local, seasonal food production comes with a consciousness about the interconnectedness of political struggles not just for women and animals, but all workers and the land itself.

The ecofeminist-vegetarian connection got its major text in 1990, when Carol J. Adams put out *The Sexual Politics of Meat*. In it, she writes about how women's oppression under patriarchy is linked with that of nonhuman animals. Women and animals both are bodies set for consumption—visual and literal—and understood to be lesser. She uses pop culture and imagery in her analysis, though the main idea she explores is the animal as the absent referent: in slaughter and consumption, the animal as a sentient being disappears. Another facet of her theory is that of "feminized protein," meaning eggs and dairy, which are produced through the reproductive cycles of the animals from which they derive; these animals live short, confined lives, and in the case of cows, their babies are taken from them and they are repeatedly inseminated to continue the production of milk intended for those calves. This is connected to the female human body, which is only presented as fulfilled through its motherly reproductive duty.

"Vegetarianism seeks meaning in a patriarchal culture that silences it," she writes in the introduction to the original edition. And while this is a political and theoretical idea, it is one that is enacted through food, classically part of the domestic and feminized sphere. This enactment of politics through food is inextricable in vegetarian and vegan food, which is why so many vegetarian cookbooks begin by telling you that they are so sorry—they don't mean to preach. Feminist vegetarians did mean to preach, and so would the punk anarchists who came after them.

Adams has also published a vegan cookbook coauthored with Virginia Messina called *Protest Kitchen: Fight Injustice, Save the Planet, and Fuel Your Resistance One Meal at a Time*, which came out in 2018, putting into practice her deeply felt ideas about vegetarian-ecofeminism being a strategy that allows people to see the oppressions of humans and nonhuman animals as interconnected. Here, they write, "A plant-based diet is a way of voicing our resistance to a political system that denies climate change and refuses to address it." The entire text is in line with the more old-school countercuisine idea that personal choices will add up to political change, but it includes concrete action ideas, addresses racial and other inequalities, and connects the way we eat each day to structural issues in society. In this book, eating is an urgent political act. Broadly speaking, though, that isn't how vegetarian and vegan diets are now perceived in the US.

How has a way of eating so long associated with counterculture hippies and ecofeminists become a mark of privilege, a sort of luxury? While feeding many people for as little money as possible has long been part of the ethos of various folks going vegetarian and vegan because it aligns with their political or spiritual ideology, there hasn't been as strong an allegiance with food-justice organizations and advocates that are working to end food apartheid in areas where fresh food has been systematically kept out. It lies in the fact that this movement didn't push the needle as far as it needed to be pushed in making organic foods accessible and affordable. In *Protest Kitchen*, Adams and Messina make these connections explicit, as Yearwood did in *The Best of Bloodroot*. It's this commitment to restating the political nature of not eating meat that pushes the conversation forward.

The natural foods that were once so difficult to find have been co-opted by corporations. Whole Foods is owned by Amazon—there can be no greater sign of there being very little political coherence between what was once countercuisine and what is now understood as healthy food. This can be seen as a win of sorts, yet the perception that vegan and vegetarian and organic foods have gone "mainstream" has been overblown. The percentage of people who identify as vegan or vegetarian or as consumers of an organics-only diet has stayed stagnant over many years, and consumer options haven't made a dent in industrial animal agriculture. In fact, consumption of beef has only increased. This is why, when I want a lesson on how to present the very real stakes of a corporate food system that is founded upon animal and worker exploitation with billions of dollars of support from the government, I go to the zines. I go to the punks.

5. PUNK GOES MAINSTREAM (SORT OF)

I've seen punk food in Buenos Aires at Donnet, a restaurant focused on mushrooms for culinary and ecological reasons. I've seen it in the Tras Talleres barrio of San Juan's Santurce neighborhood at El Departamento de la Comida. I've seen it at Foodswings, the "gone but not forgotten" Williamsburg restaurant I mentioned earlier, where protein was the center of the menu. I've heard tell of it in St. Petersburg, Russia; in Baltimore, Maryland; and Philadelphia, Pennsylvania.

A punk restaurant isn't necessarily grimy. It is often pieced together, perhaps a bit slapdash, through hand-me-down furniture and decor that doesn't quite come together in a coherent aesthetic that would make it a hit on Instagram. Certainly the lighting never helps one take a good food photo. There are some that focus, like Foodswings did, on protein—on filling people up who come in, making sure they're sated and energized to do activist work or go on tour with their band. There are others, like the organic, fair-trade, vegan chocolate shop Lagusta's Luscious and its sister restaurant Commissary! in New Paltz, New York, that are put-together, unapologetically feminine, and serve food that is hearty but composed, accessible yet well-sourced.

Punk food doesn't have to be vegan, but it usually is—it's considered a standard decision that aligns one against corporate food. This is countercuisine for Generation X, with more urgency and more in-your-face statements—basically, a countercuisine that sees where the last attempt failed. The ur-text of punk vegan food is the zine *Soy, Not "Oi!"*, which (aligning with the tradition of the vegetarian hippies and their collectively authored cookbooks) was put out by the Hippycore Krew, an extension of their punk house in Tempe, Arizona. The *New York Times* called it the vegan anarchist's *Joy of Cooking* in 2008, and indeed, it has reigned as influence and symbol.[1] "Veganism—for me at least—is a great way to say Fuck You! to the powers that be and their advertisers, as well as being an important element to an alternative, even oppositional lifestyle," wrote Joel Olson in the introduction to the AK Press reprint of the original zine.[2] The title is a reference to the musical style and movement of "Oi!," associated with Nazi skinheads, stating off the bat that these punks were against racism.

There are a lot of through lines when talking about hippie food and punk food, especially the use of the cookbook format as a place for more than just recipes—for idea-sharing, essays, and the establishment of a cohesive aesthetic for those who subscribe to the ideology. While *Soy, Not "Oi!"* was originally put out at a print run of two thousand copies in 1990, AK Press has been reprinting the zine, and it was reissued in an updated edition in 2015. I have an AK Press copy of the original, which on the back says, "Over 100 Recipes Designed to Destroy the Government," accompanied by an illustration of vegetables angrily yelling at the Capitol Building in Washington, DC. The punk position was and is firmly anarchist—thus the desire to destroy the government—and the recipes here were crowdsourced in keeping with an ethos of sharing information and resources (the Chaos Crust Tofu Chili is from someone identified simply as "Troll"). A page in a vegan "cookzine" inspired by Hippycore Krew, *Please Don't Feed the Bears!* by Brad Misanthropic, states clearly: "Copyrights are for fascists." On the back of *Raggedy Anarchy's Guide to Vegan Baking and the Universe*, it says in small, chunky handwritten letters, "copy freely."

In this way, the food was often beside the point for those compiling punk zines. As with the vegetarian cookbooks of the '70s, it was in the lifestyle that meaning resided—at least initially. For punks, that lifestyle was more rooted in refusal than in the cultivation of separatist communes. As André Gallant wrote in 2018 of his early '00s punk house days in *Southern Cultures*, in an essay called "Seasoned Punks: An Education in Cast Iron from the South's Greatest Unknown Punk Trio," going vegetarian or vegan in this subculture was about "a middle finger to a culture stuffed on burgers, an act of nonviolent protest."[3] Eating food that would have otherwise gone to the dump was another rejection of capitalism's built-in waste.

The punk perspective highlights the contradictions of what it can mean to take a political angle on vegan and vegetarian eating that is driven solely by consumerism, what has been called a "neoliberal" way of dealing with the inequalities, inefficiencies, and ecological destruction of industrial agriculture. But there's not an innate affinity between the punk-vegan viewpoint and the anarchists', despite the ways in which the ethos and symbolism tend to be used interchangeably. In "Veganism: Why Not, an Anarchist Perspective," Peter Gelderloos, an anarchist activist and author, tears down veganism on various grounds ranging from it being ineffectual to it being in alliance with capital: "Not only does veganism encourage an ignorance of market mechanisms, it also conflates consumption with agency and thus promotes a fundamental democratic myth. People are held responsible for what they buy and consume, and therefore the consumer arena is portrayed as one of free choice, rather than a violently imposed role."[4]

Regardless of how many anarchists reject veganism on philosophical grounds, the grassroots spread of a movement through recipes shows the lifestyle's function as a political tool. For punks, veganism was often the beginning of an inquiry into not just relationships with nonhuman animals and corporate food but the power of community. Zines were integral.

People like Shannon O'Neill, now an archivist at the Barnard College library, would go into the East Village's feminist bookstore Bluestockings to ask if there were new vegan zines.[5] Veganism was in natural alignment with the shop's radical ideology: it was a cooperative that opened in 1999, became worker-owned in 2001, and is still open on the Lower East Side. When I last visited, it had vegan pastries to serve alongside coffee from Zapatista cooperatives in Mexico. It was through the store's zine selection that O'Neill learned how to cook.

"Before there was a market for vegan cookbooks, zines were how I got recipes," she said. She told me this in one of the upstairs rooms of the college library, where she'd accessed some of the library's zine archive for my perusal. Its collection prioritizes the work of women and especially women of color. A search through its database for "vegan" brings up over fifty selections, covering everything from eating disorders to class to genderqueer identity.

The overlap between veganism and zine culture is a natural one. Both exist outside the mainstream, creating a space ripe for recipes printed on one side of the page and erotic poetry on the other. Zines, being self-published and self-driven, don't have to be created with sales goals in mind: a personal introduction by the author about wanting to liberate the world and herself, a story about watching a friend's home birth, and recipes for cookies and cakes all fit together, as in the aforementioned *Raggedy Anarchy's Guide to Vegan Baking and the Universe* (in which the brownie recipe is clearly influenced by *The Farm Vegetarian Cookbook*).

Noemi Martinez, the longtime zine-maker behind *Hermana Resist* and a domestic zine with recipes called *Homespun*, has been vegan since 2005. "It started at a time when I was following the work of Cesar Chavez," she said. "Since then, I've come to believe that eating vegan is more in tune with my ancestral roots and something I have to follow for spiritual growth."

That diet also aligned with her interest in zines. "I call it 'edupunk,'" she said. "My beliefs of DIY ethos and way of life, including veganism, being queer and punk were very much influenced by zines."

The interconnectedness of various movements has always been on display in zines, unlike in mainstream coverage of veganism, where it's often presented as just a diet with no political or social justice connections. "In zines, veganism seemed to come hand in hand with other radical ideas and living vegan was secondary," said Martinez, "so I could see how living vegan worked with trying to live in our society—nothing was single issue."

Gallant, the food writer based in Georgia who wrote about veganism in the punk movement, spent a short time as a hard-core vegan when introduced to it through Food Not Bombs, a network of independent collectives that gives out free meals. This work coincided with the 1990 release of *Soy, Not "Oi!"* As it was for so many others, Gallant calls it "a textbook for much of what we did."

Though he's no longer vegan, the ethos of those days influences how he continues to eat and live. "For me, the vegan food knowledge that I found in zines was part of a bigger DIY, off-the-grid, anti-capitalist ethos that pervaded the whole punk scene, but was particularly important in the South, which is where I've lived since my teens, still live today, and don't plan on leaving," he said. "Zines were snapshots of what we were eating and how we were thinking about what we were eating. Those documents connected towns just like seven-inch records did. Georgia zines went to Florida, North Carolina zines made it to Arkansas, Mississippi zines made it to Virginia. We couldn't text each other. We didn't have blogs. Zines are how we developed the ethic of being vegan and punk in the South."

Out in San Francisco, Simon Keough, publisher of the zine *Put A Egg On It*, learned of veganism while living in a punk house as a teenager where groceries were bought communally at Rainbow Grocery. "Food Not Bombs cooked out of our house once a week also and, because I was basically a runaway teen and I didn't have much money, I ate a lot of the extra stuff they left for us," they said. "My favorite thing was a bagel with vegan butter, a thin slice of raw tofu, a dash of soy sauce, and some nutritional yeast."

"There's a lot of overlap with vegans and zine culture," they said. "Anarchists, hard-core kids, sensitive queers, and animal rights activists mingled together at the same shows, same record stores, zine fairs, and bike swaps. Thinking about zines from as far back as the '80s, people were into finding their own ways to take care of themselves so you'd find personal zines talking about mental health and different kinds of self-care and also how to teach yourself to cook, cheaply and healthily. Vegan cook zines were some of the first places that taught me the basics of how to feed myself."

It can be easy to look at the zine moment as over—a relic of the '90s and '00s, as much a part of history as print magazines. But they continue to be a living form for the transmission of information outside of an explicitly capitalist publishing system. In zines, veganism's pluralistic and political nature has long been on display. Whether one dips into a library's archives or pokes around online for copies of *Please Don't Feed the Bears!*, the influence of and knowledge shared in this DIY format keep alive the dream of a vegan movement engaged in the world beyond its hunger for ice cream and seitan.

The success and influence of vegan zines and eventually online blogs contributed to what is now considered a viable glossy cookbook category—despite how much that might go against their initial anarchist ethos of sharing freely.

At first, not many vegan cookbooks were all that glossy. *How It All Vegan! Irresistible Recipes for an Animal-Free Diet* by Sarah Kramer and Tanya Barnard was initially a zine they put out in 1996 before seeing a full 1999 release from the Canadian press Arsenal Pulp. The authors' tattoos, thrift-shop dresses, and short, jet-black hairstyles were offset by retro '50s illustrations, a nod to the domesticity of it all with a knowing wink. They included a lot of recipes that harkened back to classic '70s vegetarian cookbooks like *Laurel's Kitchen* but also included what they'd learned by trial and error as young people trying to be vegan while spending most of their money on punk shows and booze rather than food. Their emphasis on using nuts as well as tofu as a means for creating fatty, eggy items like mayonnaise and basic creams is especially compelling, foreshadowing how raw vegan cuisine would come to influence non-dairy dairy. Garlic dill cream cheese, for example, calls for tofu as well as cashew pieces, a way of adding heft without adding flavor.

How It All Vegan! represented a moment for the new century. As Food Empowerment Project founder lauren Ornelas wrote, there were zines and photocopies as well as PETA and Farm Sanctuary cookbooks before 1999, but here a cultural shift occurred, allowing cooks who'd honed their skills not working in restaurants but by feeding bands passing through town or cooking with their local Food Not Bombs chapter to use their recipes, perspectives, and sense of style to define a mainstream idea of veganism deeply connected to the punk movement and animal rights. Once again, a movement that consisted of mainly men found women seeking their power through subverting the domestic arts: making it a means of independence, power, and voice rather than one of torment.

The reigning queen of punk vegan cooking in the United States since the early 2000s is undoubtedly Brooklyn-born Isa Chandra Moskowitz, a Martha Stewart for the meatless if Stewart had a lot more humor and could readily admit to not knowing the proper order in which utensils should be placed at a dinner party. She costarred in a public access cooking show in 2003 called *Post Punk Kitchen*, shot in her own apartment. The other host was Moskowitz's friend Terry Hope Romero, with whom she'd go on to author many cookbooks, including 2007's *Veganomicon*, a sprawling animal-free response to tomes like *The Joy of Cooking*. On the show, they goofed around while friends and bands came by and played; they created episodes around Valentine's Day and Passover, and made vegan sushi and tamales in other installments. It ran until 2005, when Moskowitz put out her first book: *Vegan with a Vengeance*.

In the tradition of *How It All Vegan!*, she appeared on the cover herself dressed in black, gazing upward while offering a plate of seared tofu and vegetables to the reader. *Vegan with a Vengeance* establishes Moskowitz's tone, which is knowing but easygoing (and would get a bit looser with the release of more and more cookbooks in the ensuing fifteen-plus years). The book outlines her punk roots, with recollections such as going into Manhattan in the '90s and getting into anarchism through the punk scene and making vegan food as a teenager in her mom's apartment, and then it instructs us on how to press tofu (this is where I learned the method), the eggy sulfur flavor of *kala namak*, a black salt from India, and various brunch dishes—the most difficult type of food to make vegan. ("You can't have brunch without potatoes—I'd like to see you try," starts one characteristic headnote.)

The introduction lays out what has continued to be Moskowitz's raison d'être, which was certainly radical for its time and remains so today: "It seems that many vegans depend on store-bought processed food," she writes, before noting the importance of vegans getting to know how to cook vegetables rather than being dependent on big corporations for food that comes in wasteful packaging. All of this would strike many readers as an obvious part of going vegan: if you don't want to support industrial animal agriculture, it also makes sense to cook from scratch. But Moskowitz stating it outright as a significant tenet and explaining why remains a defining moment in the evolution of vegan cooking. She later described it as the need for a "vegan cuisine" in the 2015 introduction to Miyoko Schinner's *The Homemade Vegan Pantry*.

Moskowitz has always been unabashed about her punk roots and continues to express them in her cookbooks as a means of activism, even if the books have gotten way more bells and whistles and she herself has opened two outposts of her restaurant Modern Love, in Omaha, Nebraska, and Williamsburg, Brooklyn, where her very homey style of cooking can be enjoyed without anyone having to make the seitan themselves. In the headnotes of 2016's *The Superfun Times Vegan Holiday Cookbook*—which covers everything from New Year's Eve to the Oscars to St. Patrick's Day to Hannukah—she'll often make comments like, "Who eats chicken?" that create a sort of alternate reality for vegans and vegetarians where this choice is the norm. Unlike so many vegan or vegetarian cookbooks that predate the punk aesthetic, *How It All Vegan!* and *Vegan with a Vengeance* are unapologetic about the ethical choices the authors have made. There is no manifesto to defend giving up meat, no mea culpa about "preaching"—there is just normalization and a lack of fear of the vegan "label" despite its broader cultural connotations, which could only come from cooks and authors who were fortified in their conviction by a strong political will.

While certainly the most influential to home cooks looking to go vegan or just be more vegan, Moskowitz wasn't the only significant vegan to emerge from the anarcho-punk school of thought. He's not an avowed vegan, but chef Brooks Headley went from James Beard Award–winning pastry chef at Del Posto to slinging veggie burgers at Superiority Burger (quite a punk thing to do); before he did that, though, he put out his first cookbook titled *Fancy Desserts* and included a story about hospitality that saw him and his bandmates visiting a barbecue restaurant in the American South and being served a full vegan meal. In the book itself, his silken tofu pudding pie could come straight from one of the zines of the early '90s. There's also Toad Style in Bedford-Stuyvesant, Brooklyn, which opened in 2015, and whose owners grew up in New Jersey. The punk emphasis on *doing*, on creating the world you'd like to live in, is present in all these endeavors.

Lagusta Yearwood, a chef, chocolatier, and the coauthor of Bloodroot's two "best of" collections, has been someone who's bridged the ecofeminist approach and a punk ethos in her vegan confections and cooking. She's consistently been a feminist, an anarchist, and a vegan, with a philosophy and work ethic that connects to those modes of living. Through her now-defunct blog, *Resistance Is Fertile*, I came to really understand that the farm-to-table ethos that was being fashionably espoused by chefs and food magazines wasn't antithetical to a vegan lifestyle. If Moskowitz made vegan home cooking from scratch seem doable, Yearwood made the case for a more high-gastronomy approach that championed technique, precision, and very good ingredients. The full case for her approach is present in her 2019 cookbook *Sweet + Salty: The Art of Vegan Chocolates, Truffles, Caramels, and More from Lagusta's Luscious*.

The first time I met Yearwood, in 2014, I thought I was profiling her for *Grub Street*, the food blog at the magazine where I worked at the time, *New York*. I'd been obsessed with her blog for a few years by this point, spending hours of what should've been workdays poring over the recipes and ideas, and this was how I came to understand that vegan baking was a science on its own, not just a string of substitutions. My car broke down once I got to New Paltz, New York—the college town where she still lives and works—and I didn't know what I was doing; I didn't make an audio recording of the interview, though I took copious notes in a reporter's notebook I'd taken from the magazine's supply closet. The editor eventually didn't want my piece, but I sold it to a women's website called The Hairpin (that is also now defunct, as this is how these things go). My profile of her chocolate business, Lagusta's Luscious, ran under the headline "The Punk Chocolatier"; it was the first piece of food writing I had ever published.

In the years since, I've interviewed Yearwood many more times as her business has expanded into Commissary!, a café, and Confectionery!, an East Village shop in partnership with Sweet Maresa's, a vegan bakery that began in Lagusta's Luscious and made its mark as the first to perfect eggless macarons. Confectionery! is located close to Superiority Burger; together they've created a vegan corner in the gentrifying city—a stronghold to feed anyone still skateboarding and hanging out in Tompkins Square Park. When I asked, in an interview for the magazine *Good Company*, whether the expansions scared her, Yearwood said, "I think this is the theme of my whole life: If I'd thought about it, I would've been scared. I actually just got fear in my stomach thinking about how scary it was. We were like, 'We'll just rent a place in Manhattan and open a shop.' You just do one thing after another and look back and see that they were extremely terrifying. Anything I've ever done in business, I've never known the right way to do it, so I just did it and, amazingly, that has worked out so far. I'm glad about it, because how else would you do things?"[6]

That she leads with her gut—in more ways than one—as well as her politics and commitment to creating inclusive spaces, support to great suppliers, and good jobs, has clear origins in the collective and punk approach, based on following one's instincts and gathering inspiration and support from one's community. Ever since my first visit to her shop, I have followed her trajectory and been in awe of its cohesion.

"Women! Let us meet." This is how Yearwood called together her employees for a staff meeting on that first visit. (It would have made the Bloodroot women happy, I think now.) Four women then stood around Yearwood, all in vintage aprons, listening as she discussed the business of the day: a new whipped cream recipe, strategies for most efficiently using the Enrober to get 1,400 caramels out. Over to the side, I noted a "Kill Your Local Misogynists" mug. This space was all my food-world fantasies come to life; it still makes me very anxious to talk to Yearwood, because she has achieved such a seemingly impossible task: be a successful woman in food while maintaining transparency and rigorous radical politics. In the subsequent interviews over the years after my first visit, she was adamant that she not be the only member of the team interviewed.

After getting a degree in women's studies, Yearwood attended New York City's Natural Gourmet Institute and trained in Connecticut at Bloodroot. She began her foray into being what she calls an "antipreneur" with a service delivering savory food. It was during off-hours while running that business that she began rolling and selling fair-trade-chocolate truffles out of her home. In 2010, she bought the foreclosed laundromat that would become Lagusta's Luscious, envisioning it as a wholesale chocolate factory with a shop up front for selling extras. Instead, at that time, the split between retail and mail order sales was about 60–40, respectively.

Lagusta's Luscious doesn't advertise, and she herself had been at the forefront of their social media presence: claiming fruit as her religion, writing poetic treatises in Instagram captions, railing against what many mainstream chefs conceive of as a vegan meal on her personal blog. She made Sliding Scale Socialist Soup, for which customers pay what they can, and turned down potential deals with big companies because of their shady corporate practices.

The shop itself is tiny, with a teal and brown color scheme, as well composed in its shabby-twee aesthetic as her chocolates are in flavor;

they're now expanding into a new space. The counter was made from reclaimed wood and bartered for with a local artisan; the lampshades were made by a friend. The bathroom is wallpapered in leftist political posters, including one, hanging over the toilet, of Ronald McDonald with a Hitler 'stache. It's a place where workers are paid a living wage and taken on field trips to restaurants and other chocolate-makers to develop their palates. It's a place where a tween girl asks for a Furious Vulva in her assortment, please, without a giggle or a smirk.

Yearwood comes from a vegan activist background, but it's emotionally exhausting work. She sees participating in capitalism as better than her business not existing, as we "don't have 20 years to wait for a radical revolution." In the meantime, she uses ecofriendly packaging, cuts waste wherever possible, and works with similarly minded businesses and artisans. Along with the economic issues, there's being the boss of eight people when one is not really down with hierarchy. Providing jobs, though, is a point of pride, as is allowing all the employees to find where they fit in best. She's forgotten how to wrap her own chocolate bars and is no longer dipping every truffle herself; such things are handled by the people she's trained exceptionally well, and she's learned to be okay with that.

But the chocolates. They are what make the whole endeavor worthwhile and what truly set the shop apart. There are very few simple pieces in the case. There's a Sour Sorrel Caramel in the spring, made with the exceptional, sharply flavored herb. Sorrel caramel is enrobed in chocolate and garnished with a matcha-mint salt. It's odd and lovely, fresh and rich. A favorite of most is the Vandana Shiva, named for the anti-GMO seed activist. It's made from stone-ground chocolate, which gives it an earthy texture, and flavored with mild ancho chilies, Maui vanilla beans, and Mexican cinnamon. The Furious Vulva the tween asked for is formed in a vulva mold—helpfully reminding us all that a vagina is what's on the inside—with pink peppercorns and Hawaiian pink sea salt. It's a bit sassy, a lot cute, and a delicate match of spice and bitterness.

When I asked her about the risk of making so many palate-challenging flavors, she mentioned the Almond and Dark Chocolate Bark with Smoked Sea Salt. "It's never something I'll nibble on," but it sells and perhaps serves as a gateway.

Yearwood holds herself to a high standard by sourcing only high-quality ingredients, coming up with intricate flavors, and keeping local what can be local; this is not just a contrast to how mainstream food businesses work, but a major anomaly among vegan offerings. There is no slick, palm oil–based Earth Balance here. The chocolate itself, now sourced from República del Cacao, is unapologetically dark.

"They're impressed with anything," Yearwood said of vegans, and it's true. Make a cute cupcake and folks are just grateful to have something to put in their mouths, no matter the actual texture or flavor. But when someone moves beyond simply providing something animal product–free and into doing exceptional culinary work, it expands the possibilities of the movement. If you know that going vegan doesn't mean dooming yourself to a life of dry cookies and rubbery fake cheese, you're more likely to make the leap. It's activism through hedonism, proving what's possible even when cutting animal protein, and using local, organic, and fair-trade ingredients.

More in her wheelhouse is the Pig Out Bar, made from infusing a caramel sauce with house-smoked shiitake mushrooms and red miso as well as smoked yuba, a by-product of the soy milk–making process. It created a smoky, bacon-y goodness without relying on ubiquitous liquid smoke. She bought the smoker in order to develop the richest pig-less bacon she could and looked at the actual bacon-making process online, which involved holding her hand up to the screen to block out gruesome imagery.

"I really wanted to know, How do you get these flavors?" she told me in 2018. "Obviously it's dead animal flesh, but other than that, there's something done to make it be this thing. And I feel like it's almost like this game of telephone where everything in the vegan world gets reduced down to like, *Oh, bacon is smoky, OK, so add liquid smoke, you're done*. Like, anything becomes bacon if you just add something that's like a little smoky. That's not how the non-vegan world works, and no one would let that fly. And so I think like we have to hold ourselves to this higher standard, because everyone makes fun of vegans already."

It's difficult to envision her kind of craftsmanship working on a massive scale, though, and that's been the struggle facing the shop as it grows. "I try really hard to not care about making a profit—which is obvious because I don't really make a profit—and I'm always trying to push my politics into things," she explained to me in 2018. "What's the point of being alive if you're not doing weird shit? My whole business philosophy is, 'How weird can I make it? How far can I push it?'"

Though the chocolate shop would theoretically fit in perfectly on New Paltz's main street, among the organic grocers and yoga studios, it's a bit hidden on a back road, an almost too-perfect metaphor for its place in the world. Not content to hang out even with who you'd think are its peers, Lagusta's Luscious needs its smallness and solitude to continue being this radical bastion of weird chocolates and delicious mac and cheese.[7]

From *Soy, Not "Oi!"* to *Veganomicon* to the fair-trade truffles of Lagusta's Luscious, there's been an unapologetic bent to how openly punk vegans have wanted to share their knowledge and their food in the hopes of creating a better world. While their culinary lineage borrows from counterculture cookbooks and non-Western vegetarian tradition, their perspectives have taken a philosophy and made it edible—and they've turned it into a cuisine recognizable around the world, wherever someone would be happy to feed you or your band for five dollars. Punk veganism is a politics of hospitality, at its core, rooted in the home and expanding ever outward into cookbooks, restaurants, and cafés that serve food that seeks to nourish, entertain, and maybe—just maybe—get one more person off industrial animal agriculture.

6. MEATLESS PLURALITY

Not eating meat, whether as a vegetarian, vegan, or plant-based flexitarian, does not come with a standard food-justice playbook. As I've been writing, in the United States, these approaches to food have been popularized in the imagination and immortalized in the famous cookbooks by mainly white folks of the baby boomer generation, and that has left its political perspective and justice orientation adrift. They're open to interpretation and there is no pledge of allegiance, meaning there have been troubling strains of thought allowed to fester under the umbrella of animal welfare and perhaps not enough focus on broader, more community- and policy-oriented approaches to food justice and access.

There are even conservative vegans. In the United Kingdom, they have their own caucus in the Conservative Party. In the United States, Matthew Scully has been the most vocal conservative proponent of animal rights. His 2002 book, *Dominion: The Power of Man, the Suffering of Animals, and the Call to Mercy*, argues for an end to factory farming and hunting, stating that animals are worthy of human care and concern because of their powerlessness. A speechwriter for various politicians in both the Democrat and Republican parties, including former president George W. Bush, he is the kind of conservative who called themselves pro-life while supporting the war in Iraq, which killed an estimated two hundred thousand civilians.[1] A

New York Times "Vows" column in 2018 told of the meeting of two conservative vegan lawyers.[2]

While they go against the common understanding of meat being a non-negotiable tenet of right-wing ideology, conservative veganism makes a sort of sense philosophically to the practitioners: to them, animals are sentient and sacred, and so is the conservation of the environment of which animals are a part. If it strikes one as sensible that care for animals and the environment should also extend to vulnerable people and a deeply cruel and discriminatory carceral system, I agree.

But there is an even uglier strain of right-wing veganism that's called "ecofascism." Those who subscribe to this way of thinking argue that climate change will result in resource scarcity, and they thus must prioritize the well-being of their own people—namely, white people who claim the Global North as home. For the ecofascists, this means turning away migrants from the Global South who are already suffering the effects of a warming planet.

As Sarah Manavis wrote in 2018 for the *New Statesman* while examining the phenomenon of ecofascism and its connection to white supremacy and veganism, "Many eco-fascists are also eugenicists who believe that a culling of the population, and specific races within that population, is the only way to ensure that the planet survives. While not all eco-fascists go as far as supporting mass murder, most hold that immigration has caused overpopulation in their countries and insists that the only solution is to deport those they deem non-indigenous."[3]

Ecofascism thinking is underpinned by the work of Thomas Robert Malthus, an English economist born in 1766 who believed that population growth would always outrun the global food supply and that limits on reproduction were a necessary condition of "human betterment." His influence is known as Malthusianism, and it saw a rebirth in the 1960s with the publication of *The Population Bomb* by Paul R. Ehrlich, which influenced Frances Moore Lappé to get herself to the library and produce the book that was *Diet for a Small Planet*—completed while she was pregnant—to prove Ehrlich and Malthus wrong. The human population would not outstretch food supply if food production occurred in a sane way and not, as she famously put it, as "a protein factory in reverse."

In her analysis of population as a "problem," Lappé always focused on where power and resources were concentrated, encouraging changes to socioeconomic and power structures that would create better options for people in their own communities. In a 1988 study for the organization Food First, Lappé and coauthor Rachel Schurman wrote that the "lack of a clear link between population density and hunger is a strong rebuttal to the people-versus-resources conception of the problem." They demonstrated the lack of a link by comparing the hunger levels of countries with similar population density, proving that "many other factors beyond sheer numbers obviously determine whether people eat adequately."[4] That's where social, economic, and access issues come into play, which is why ecofascism and neo-Malthusian ideas about population only make sense if one is coming from a racist framework where one population is more desirable than another and its growth is thus considered "advantageous."

In short, this realization that social and economic factors relating to food access significantly affect what people eat and its nutritional value is where food justice emerges, and food justice is entangled with a more plant-based way of eating. In recent years, there has been growing concern about these issues, as well as an active effort to diversify who is thought of as a vegan, vegetarian, or plant-based person. But what is food justice? FoodPrint, an organization that compiles reports on sustainability, defines food justice as "a holistic and structural view of the food system that sees healthy food as a human right and addresses structural barriers to that right."[5] The concept has been adapted from the idea of environmental justice, which, in the 1980s, came about as a way of responding to the environmental movement's increasing whiteness, elitism, and focus on wilderness. Instead, environmental justice sought to respond to how vulnerable communities were affected by pollution.

Food justice, then, seeks to respond to similar tendencies in the broader food movement, whose popular focus had been getting more people of means to eat local, organic produce and be concerned with labels such as "fair trade." Those are good things, but they do not tackle the root issues of the people most affected by low-wage work and food apartheid. A food-justice perspective doesn't just see healthy food as a human right, it sees culturally appropriate food as a human right—meaning that it would not force upon a community a kind of food that doesn't make sense for that people's way of eating. This approach means engaging with the very people who are most affected by a lack of access to nutritious foods, and letting their needs and desires lead changes to the food system.

Plant-based eating is part of a food-justice perspective because over-reliance on industrial meat and fast food has been a driver of diet-related disease in communities where fresh food is not prevalent. Culturally appropriate and accessible foods based on whole grains and legumes would be the point at which food justice and plant-based cuisine intersect. The process by which meatless eating and food justice have become a more coherent and cohesive movement has been manifold; the vegan and vegetarian community has grown and diversified thanks to social media allowing more voices into the fold, and that increased diversity of thought and perspective has been arising alongside more mainstream visibility of plant-based cooks, thinkers, and organizations who are contributing to a forward-thinking, justice-oriented approach to changing how people think about this movement and way of eating.

A big part of what has changed in the plant-based space has been the publication of cookbooks from various non-European cuisines that normalize a lack of animal products. Although, in the past, vegetarian cookbooks by Chinese or Indian authors made occasional appearances on shelves, these cuisines also made up major parts of the cookbooks by white authors. Authoritative, in-depth, and personal deep dives into various cuisines and the ways they could de-center meat from the plate were not as commonplace.

While vegetarian cookbooks today don't exhibit the level of diversity achieved in omnivorous cuisines, there is still far wider representation in both cuisines and authorship—despite the fact that publishing as a whole remains 76 percent white, 74 percent cis women, 81 percent straight, and 89 percent non-disabled.[6] As cookbook author Julia Turshen wrote for *Eater* in 2018, "Authors of color are often represented by white agents who are pitching to white editors and white publishers. Authors of color are often the only person of color in the rooms where decision making happens."[7]

A 2020 *New York Times* piece on an increase in the number of cookbook deals going to Black authors cautioned against too much optimism, saying, "Many Black writers and chefs say there has long been an unspoken limit on the number of books that are produced about Black food, compared with a seemingly bottomless appetite for titles on French or Italian cuisine. Some feel typecast or stereotyped by the cooking styles expected of them. . . . There have also been concerns about whether Black writers are paid as much as their white peers."[8]

These issues have a huge impact on what and who is published; the financial factor, as well as the fact that agents and editors may not fully comprehend non-European concepts and techniques, creates added labor for many authors of color. Stories abound in food media of microaggressions toward anything that could be considered "other," with writers of color having to fight and explain themselves far more than white writers, who have been able to cover subjects with far more range and diversity. Writer Osayi Endolyn told the *New Yorker* in 2021 that, despite identity not necessarily being a marker of expertise, "There's a sense in editorial, publishing, and TV spaces that, if you are from a nonwhite background, what you talk about has to be generated from your identity in some way. But if you're a white person you can go anywhere you want. You can talk about Asian cuisines, you can talk about African or African American cuisines, you can talk about South American cuisines."[9]

That there are some new faces and rampant successes for explicitly vegan cookbook authors right now is a marked change that will hopefully usher in more of the same, and it is a reason for cautious optimism that suggests the dawn of a new day for how vegans and vegetarians are pictured in the mainstream—perhaps with nonwhite vegans no longer considered niche, but simply part of a grand historical and growing tradition.

Joanne Lee Molinaro's *The Korean Vegan Cookbook: Reflections and Recipes from Omma's Kitchen*, a *New York Times* bestseller as well as the best-selling plant-based cookbook of 2021 according to Amazon sales, takes from the author's own upbringing, experience, and cooking style, which she adapted to her meatless diet and popularized through social media. *The Modern Tiffin: On-the-Go Vegan Dishes with a Global Flair* by Priyanka Naik also came out in 2021 to great success; in the book, Naik includes fifty-five recipes from around the world, showcasing the adaptability of plant-based food to the global pantry and giving support to the reality that nonwhite cookbook authors shouldn't be pigeonholed by their identity when their expertise is broad.

One of the most famous vegan cookbook authors has long been Bryant Terry, who came onto the scene with the cookbook *Vegan Soul Kitchen* in 2009, following a collaboration with Anna Lappé (Frances's daughter) in 2006 called *Grub: Ideas for an Urban Organic Kitchen*. Their coauthored cookbook points out "the six illusions" that Americans are living with regarding food: "choice," "cheap," "safe and clean," "fairness," "efficiency," and "progress."[10] They argue that the diet of most people in the US is not nourishing; rather, it's making them ill. Although most supermarkets can provide winter strawberries, economies of locally grown, fresh food have died. As a food-justice text, Lappé and Terry's work merges the practical and the political in a way that both would continue to do with urgency and, in Terry's case, artistry. All his cookbooks also feature playlists, weaving a cultural fabric that presents plant-based food as part of bigger Black traditions and giving his food a foundation upon which to stand. Perhaps you don't like mushrooms yet, but you do like Juicy J.

In these connections, Terry forges common ground and commits to legibility, no matter what level one's experience with the chiffonade technique of chopping leafy greens might be.

His uniqueness as a voice in the food world has been established over twenty years: Terry's first foray into food was as the founder of b-healthy in 2002, an initiative he ran in New York City to empower youth to fight for a sustainable food system and recognize the connection between their personal health and the socioeconomic situations of their communities.

Put simply, Terry has always taken a deep historical and intersectional approach to food justice and plant-based cooking; he has a master's in history from NYU and studied at the Natural Gourmet Institute. His work has a culinary and cultural history edge because of his rigorous approach, and that approach has been rewarded with accolades as well as his own imprint at Ten Speed Press called 4 Color Books—something that will make a distinct difference for cookbook authors of color working in this exceedingly white industry.

Black Food, the imprint's sprawling debut, edited by Terry, is a continuation of his work as well as of counterculture and political cookbooks that combine recipes with essays—that ever-necessary melding of the practical reality of cooking with the political ideas that are always already underpinning that act, whether we believe it's there or not. It isn't a vegan book, but that makes the inclusion of plant-based recipes and essays on the subject all the more effective, including a contribution from the likes of Tracye McQuirter, MPH, author of 2010's *By Any Greens Necessary: A Revolutionary Guide for Black Women Who Want to Eat Great, Get Healthy, Lose Weight, and Look Phat*. They're not dominant, nor are they presented as "other"; their presence is accepted alongside the fish, the braised goat. The buttermilk biscuit recipe from chef Erika Council is immediately followed by her vegan sweet potato coconut biscuits. Vegetables, grains, and legumes abound. It is a text that shows precisely how it is possible to move forward toward plant-based normalization, and it shows it through the expansive experiences of the African diaspora.

As Terry told me during our 2020 conversation:

I would say my understanding of cooking being a political act is what really moved me to engage in food-justice activism.

Before I got into the food world, I was actually a doctoral student at NYU, and my advisor was a brilliant historian named Robin D.G. Kelley. His second scholarly monograph . . . is called *Race Rebels*. Basically what he does is, he's kind of looking at methods of resistance adopted by Black working-class folks in the 20th century to resist capitalism and white supremacy. He talks about things like slow-downs, quitting on the spot, leaving work early—really the subversive acts that were the unorganized ways that many people would resist these systems of oppression. There's also more organized labor unions and things like that. That book helped me to develop this kind of bifocal approach where I'm thinking about larger systems and structures but also acknowledging and uplifting these kinds of everyday acts of resistance.

When I think about something like cooking or gardening or, you know, building community with family around the table, I think a lot of people might see these as apolitical. I would argue in our industrialized world that's controlled by a handful of multinational corporations that are invested in you shopping at these corporate-owned supermarkets or eating at fast-food restaurants or stuffing your face really quickly so you can get back to work, I would argue that making meals from scratch, growing your own food, gathering around the table are highly political and, dare I say, radical. In and of themselves, they're not enough to continue to transform our food system, but I think they need to be uplifted alongside more organized forms of radical resistance to these oppressive systems.

While cookbook deals and social media follower counts do not create an entirely new food system on their own, they are indicators—more than an increase in plant-based processed foods in the grocery store, I'd say—of an increasing normalization and expansion of vegan cuisine. On the theory side, there has also been a shift toward stories of Black women vegans, queer vegans, Indigenous vegans, differently abled vegans, and others that has become undeniably visible—and that visibility, combined with increasing culinary normalcy, means a cultural shift. Perhaps there aren't more people identifying as vegan, but there are more people who know what it is. And while they may know what a vegan is only through exposure to insulting memes about vegans, there are far more examples to point to of people who are pushing back on the notions of the pedantic, preachy white vegan that has dominated the mainstream discourse.

Reviewing *By Any Greens Necessary* in *Food and Foodways*, scholar Ashanté M. Reese writes, "At best, veganism is a way of eating, a way of life that seemingly has nothing to do with race. At worst, it is a way of eating, a way of life tied to whiteness."[11] Undoing this association has taken considerable effort.

One of the most significant thinkers on the topic of Black veganism is A. Breeze Harper, the editor of *Sistah Vegan: Black Women Speak on Food, Identity, Health, and Society*, which originally came out in 2010. Harper writes in a foreword to a tenth anniversary edition released in 2020 about the ways in which Black, Indigenous, and people of color "struggle with multiple issues that cannot be detached from one another"; this intersectionality allows for a multifaceted approach to veganism.[12] Harper notes that community activists are "more aware of how [food and nutrition] relate to decolonizing the systems that have been set in place to hurt racial minorities." In giving up animal products, they are going back to their "cultural food roots, but veganized," as a way of thinking about how white supremacy has historically animalized Black people, which leads in turn to an analysis of nonhuman animal suffering.

The animalization of marginalized people is a consistent point in vegan thought. It is part of Carol J. Adams's ecofeminist framework, which likens the consumption of meat to the consumption of the female body under patriarchy, and it is integral to Sunaura Taylor's analysis in her 2017 book *Beasts of Burden: Animal and Disability Liberation*, in which she writes of the ways in which differently abled people are considered less than, in much the same way nonhuman animals, are to point out that the categories of "human" and "animal" are socially rather than just biologically constructed. Taylor's analysis especially looks at how industrially farmed animals become disabled under their cramped and unnatural conditions, as well as how they are bred over time to become cows that produce more milk than their udders can hold, pigs with legs too weak for them to stand upon, and chickens with such large breasts that they cannot bear their weight. She writes of how these disabling characteristics and their impact on the health of the animals is discussed only in terms of cost, which correlates with how disability is discussed as an expensive burden on society.

The Indigenous scholar Margaret Robinson wrote in "Veganism and Mi'kmaq Legends," "Meat, as a symbol of patriarchy shared with colonizing forces, arguably binds us with white colonial culture to a greater degree than practices such as veganism, which, although overwhelmingly white itself, is far from hegemonic."[13] In *Veganism in an Oppressive World: A Vegans-of-Color Community Project*, a 2017 book edited by Julia Feliz Bruek, Bruek expands on Robinson's work to explain why veganism has historically been looked upon as a privileged white movement that doesn't understand the realities of intersecting identities. Robinson sees this as a core issue in veganism at large; when one looks at veganism through a food justice–oriented lens, it is consistently clear that the white-dominated movement is one that doesn't fully engage with poverty and food apartheid, structural realities that by design keep fresh, affordable food out of reach in many communities.

Over the years, from the counterculture communes through the ecofeminist collectives and punk houses, vegetarian and vegan food have been coded as white by the mainstream—and indeed, in these subcultures, most participants were white; the most visible and best-selling cookbooks in this realm have historically also been by white writers. In addition, animal rights philosophy historically has been dominated by able-bodied, cisgender white straight men, but, crucially, the status quo has changed in the last decade, as more people of color and those of marginalized identities claim an intersectional perspective on animal rights. Personal narrative has also become more significant as a means of understanding the human relationship to nonhuman animals, which has a diversifying effect on the voices as well. The tendencies of zines and counterculture cookbooks to bring in essays, poetry, and aphorism have become more accepted, and with that, our understanding of the many facets of meatless experience expands. A prismatic and intersectional understanding is the only way forward.

These changes, in the culture and cuisine of plant-based food as well as the related texts, have had to be combined with a food-justice lens in order to shape a food future without industrial animal agriculture. Food Empowerment Project has been an organization carrying that full load forward, with multilingual cuisine projects such as VeganMexicanFood.com, VeganFilipinoFood.com, and VeganLaoFood.com, making plant-based approaches to traditional cuisines accessible. When it does assessments of access to fresh food in various communities, Food Empowerment Project conducts focus groups with members of those communities themselves to understand the precise barriers, which are then brought to local governments. Its reports have been cited by the United Nations Human Rights Committee. The organization also does studies of cacao sourcing for vegan chocolates and advocates for farmworkers in local government, along with supporting their children with school supply drives. Whereas other vegan nonprofits are one-dimensionally focused on animal rights, the missions of Food Empowerment Project set the organization apart by focusing on the conditions that make people reliant on a diet based in processed foods, fast food, and industrially produced meat and dairy.

The need to diversify the movement isn't the only factor behind the move toward a food justice–oriented veganism; it owes a lot to those who have been working on these issues and making these connections for decades. Black veganism has roots in the civil rights movement and various religious groups and faiths, such as the Nation of Islam and Rastafarianism, and younger vegans have taken the lessons imparted from these elder practitioners; Aph Ko launched a website in 2015 featuring a list of 100 Black vegans as a way of rooting the movement historically.

Jenné Claiborne, chef and author of *Sweet Potato Soul*, told the *New York Times* in 2017, "For a lot of black people, it's also [about] the social justice and food access. The food we have been eating for decades and decades and has been killing us."[14] A health-oriented veganism among Black, brown, and Indigenous people is different from a wellness perspective focused on thinness and individual care. Instead, it champions a way of eating that has demonstrated it can alleviate and prevent diet-related disease.

Over the last fifty years, the cooking and culture of meatless cuisine in the US has evolved, and diversity has come to be a defining aspect of its strength. Though many measure plant-based foods' success by the number of processed items in stores—and that is one way of looking at it—I see the merging of the culinary and cultural thought as a crucial moment in meatless history, one that could define its future.

7. WHEATGRASS AND WELLNESS

"The good smells of your food cooking are the nutrients leaving," the yoga instructor told us as we contorted our bodies. This line has stayed with me for so long, like a haunting. Could it be true? Could there be something to the raw foodists' ideas about health, about oil clogging my intestines and cooked grains similarly gumming up the works? I was vegan at the time, eating as healthy as I thought possible—and probably not getting enough calories anyway—and still I considered that I wasn't doing enough to make sure my body was reaching its highest point of purity. Why would I want that, though? Why was purity a goal?

What has always kept me from going fully off the deep end in terms of the fatphobic, body-shaming wellness strain that nags veganism (not so much vegetarianism, as steeped as its reputation is in the butter and sour cream of the early Moosewood days) is that I love to eat. That was the gift my grandma gave me before she passed, and I have remained true to it, though I am not as curious as she was about the taste of frog legs—for which she brought five children on a road trip from Long Island to Quebec City. No, I go in search of fruits, vegetables, fried tempeh, and the perfect Neapolitan pizza. For a time, though, I did also seek out zucchini-based noodles and cold cashew cheese.

I became vegan through a yoga practice where raw veganism was preached, where juice cleanses were encouraged. I tried a juice cleanse once, and I didn't make it to liquid lunch, and the nagging feeling to me that this was starvation and not healthy eating was backed up by nutrition science. Smoothies, where the fibers of fruits and vegetables are retained, were preferable to cold-pressed juices, but it was the latter that I was being sold and told to consume. I kept trying, though, to find better health through raw food, even going to a café on Long Island that sold only "living foods," where I bought a "lasagna" based on those cold zucchini noodles and filled with a cold, bland cashew cheese. Again, I couldn't finish.

Being naturally thin has saved me from the stigma of size, but even at my skinniest—as I was during this yoga period of measuring olive oil by the tablespoon and drinking smoothies—there was a current of fatphobia and health shaming running through the vegan circles in which I was part. Which isn't to say it was or is all bad, but the focus on "health" in vegetarian and vegan communities and cookbooks has often mirrored bigger public health messaging around what is called "obesity" but could be more accurately referred to as diet-related disease. Health, even when understood as a public good, is individualized (we saw this play out ceaselessly in the pandemic, as the ability to obtain masks, sick days for vaccines, and access to tests was left up to an individual's decision-making, type of job, and wealth level). Fatness becomes important because of the perception of it as a matter of people's individual choices and willpower, thus washing the state and various communities' hands of any need for structural changes that would truly improve health outcomes. Fatphobia is also a systemic means of discrimination with material outcomes, one with roots in white supremacy, as argued by Sabrina Strings in *Fearing the Black Body: The Racial Origins of Fat Phobia*; Strings calls fatphobia a means of justifying a host of biases, from racial to economic to gender-based.

In the introduction to an issue of the journal *Fat Studies* on public health, published in early 2022, Nina Mackert and Friedrich Schorb write about the ways in which the individual is the sole addressee when it comes to the discussion of risk factors against chronic disease.

This unfolds through public health campaigns that focus on taxes on items deemed unhealthy such as soda products. These individual-level changes, though, are not attacking root causes of people's poor health. As Mackert and Schrob write: "At the far end of the spectrum of likely recommendations are measures that focus on in-depth societal changes, like the improvement of working conditions, the provision of universal health care, the creation of income equality, and the eradication of poverty. The latter measures are most effective in improving health on a large scale, but they are also harder to link to specific changes in the prevalence of concrete diseases and they do attract fierce political opposition."[1]

A justice-oriented and body positive plant-based movement would focus on the latter structural changes rather than individual decision-making as the most significant factors that determine rates of diet-related disease in a society, such as diabetes and heart conditions. Juice cleanses and hot yoga classes are expensive and time-consuming, and they let the state off the hook for poverty wages and a lack of adequate and accessible health care.

Historically, though, the plant-based movement, as a consumer boycott of animal agriculture, has not had a politically minded orientation when it comes to getting people onboard. It has mirrored the mainstream messaging around public health as a matter of individual choice, and promoted the idea that dietary change away from animal protein can lead to thinness. While health and nutrition are of course significant aspects of what we eat, why have meatless diets been so susceptible to obsessive health-washing?

It could stem from defensiveness, as popular wisdom in broader US society suggests the only way to be healthy and strong is to consume meat and other animal proteins, which is why so many vegan magazines love to promote the strength of plant-based athletes and bodybuilders. Corey Lee Wrenn, in a 2017 article titled "Fat Vegan Politics: A Survey of Fat Vegan Activists' Online Experiences with Social Movement Sizeism" for the journal *Fat Studies*, wrote, "Vegans engage fat-shaming as a means of protecting veganism as a viable and positive lifestyle, while also promising weight loss and a conventionally attractive body to adherents in hopes of controlling the attitudes and behaviors of its nonvegan audience."[2]

The urge to protect veganism as a worthwhile and healthful endeavor is a natural response to years of bad press. In *The Vegan Studies Project: Food, Animals, and Gender in the Age of Terror*, Laura Wright, an English professor at Western Carolina University, writes about "the vegan body" as a contested site in American culture, especially after 9/11. This was a cultural moment when American strength was supposedly under attack, and the vegan body became a focal point for its refusal to bow to norms of eating, dressing, and dominating animals. In the chapter "Death by Veganism," she looks into studies and specious claims around vegan parenting, connections between veganism and disordered eating, and why an animal rights agenda is masked in books like *Skinny Bitch: A No-Nonsense, Tough-Love Guide for Savvy Girls Who Want to Stop Eating Crap and Start Looking Fabulous!* by Rory Freedman and Kim Barnouin. Wright writes, "For women, dieting is always an acceptable body project, even as women's dietary choices are so closely scrutinized. Veganism, however, is suspect, subversive, and dangerous."[3]

Skinny Bitch combined animal rights and wellness culture by including chapters on factory farming and animal cruelty, but also advocated abstaining from refined sugar, alcohol, caffeine, and "chemical additives." Thus, though a bestseller in the US and UK, the fact that they strongly emphasized restriction and a socially acceptable thin body didn't really help the vegan cause.

That thin vegan body has also been one of the chief selling points of the nutritionally questionable raw foods diet, which was established at the end of the nineteenth century by Maximilian Bircher-Benner, a Swiss doctor. He opened a sanitarium in the Swiss Alps in 1904, where people were fed a raw diet that he saw as retaining the foods' "Life Force" from solar energy, which could be removed by cooking. (More than a century later, it would be the same argument I'd hear in yoga class for going raw.)

This philosophy made its way to the US via Ann Wigmore, a Lithuanian woman who married a man from Massachusetts, which is where she would establish her church, Rising Sun Christianity, in 1963, which eventually became the Hippocrates Health Institute in 1982. Finding an authoritative biography of Wigmore isn't easy. Her acolytes have clogged up search results to speak of the "detox" power of wheatgrass juice shots, and those on the other end of the spectrum regard her as not worthy of anything more than a laugh for her quackery. What is funny is that any juice bar you walk into even today will have a trough of wheatgrass growing, because Wigmore believed its juice had such a short life span that it had to be cut, juiced, and consumed in quick succession. Also, much artisanal, fermented vegan nut cheese owes its initial existence to the ease of Wigmore's rejuvelac recipe, which calls for sprouting wheat berries into a lightly fermented beverage. Early nut cheese recipes called for using this fermented liquid to "culture" nut milk, and it would go on to become integral in the development of vegan cheese.

Sprouts, another of her obsessions, are in the produce section of any supermarket. The *Vegetarian Times* called her a genius in 1990, three years after she put out the book *Overcoming AIDS and Other "Incurable Diseases" the Attunitive Way Through Nature*, which invited a lawsuit from the Massachusetts attorney general because of the claims in a recipe for an enzyme soup that would, she wrote, "build back the immune system."[4] A judge decided this was protected free speech. Today, the Hippocrates Health Institute still exists in Florida and the Ann Wigmore Natural Health Institute is open in Aguada, Puerto Rico.

She wouldn't be the first figure who came to vegan foods through odd health claims, as it was the same for John Harvey Kellogg, who at the Battle Creek Sanitarium advocated for similar notions of "purity" in diet, mind, and spirit—in his case, influenced by Seventh-Day Adventism rather than new age ideas. But because she lied about her credentials and made unsubstantiated claims about curing disease with raw foods, her legacy in the vegan movement is complex, to say the least. People still shell out money for treatments that don't work because of legal loopholes around what precisely the Hippocrates Health Institute says about their effects. Brian Clement, who took over as head of the institute in Palm Beach following Wigmore's 1994 death, was ordered to cease and desist practicing medicine after an eleven-year-old girl died under his care—of a leukemia that has a 98 percent chance of remission through Western medicine.[5] Despite the "genius" of sprouts, Wigmore's most lasting legacy is one of fraud and quackery. One doesn't want to discount the health benefits of cutting meat out of a diet and cutting back on animal products, whether totally or mostly, but it also means contending with a not-so-distant past in which this way of eating was aligned with very questionable preoccupations and claims.

Despite the lack of evidence for health claims about raw food and the lawsuits for quackery Wigmore was served with, raw vegan food experienced a surge of popularity in the 1990s and 2000s, which persists through juice bars if not fully raw restaurants. It was in the late '90s when raw vegan foods emerged as a full style of cooking, with restaurants and cookbooks; these books still made many health claims about raw foods, none of them very precise or clear—just things like feelings of "lightness" and "vitality," as Matt Fitzgerald chronicled in his 2014 book *Diet Cults: The Surprising Fallacy at the Core of Nutrition Fads and a Guide to Eating Healthy for the Rest of Us.*

California, as usual, was an origin point. A man who went by the mononym Juliano opened a thirty-five-seat restaurant called Raw Living Foods in San Francisco, which he had changed to Organica by the time his cookbook *Raw: The UNcookbook* came out in 1999 and the *San Francisco Chronicle* visited. It wasn't the first time: Michael Bauer, the paper's traditional restaurant critic, gave Raw Living Foods what amounted to a rave review with two stars in 1995, writing, "The food is never going to compete with Chez Panisse, but any true gourmand should go at least once and be amazed at the variety of flavors and combinations Juliano can coax from the food."[6]

According to Juliano's origin story, he grew up in Las Vegas, the child of an Italian restaurateur. Connecting with nature as a teenager led to him becoming vegetarian, and then vegan, and then raw. (Though he went by his first name for years, his last name would become known: Brotman.) His mother invested $50,000 in the opening of his restaurant, which then attracted a celebrity clientele that included Woody Harrelson and Robin Williams. The *Raw* book tells his secrets, which, like much raw food, involve sprouting grains and legumes, soaking nuts and dates, dehydrating leftover juice pulp and seeds into "crackers," calling plain avocado "green cream cheese," and spiking nuts with rejuvelac for a cheesy bite. In the text he's evangelical about the superiority of a raw foods lifestyle, calling roasted seeds "dead," though Bauer quotes him in his review as saying, "People can go out for Chinese one night, Thai the next and then on another night go out for raw."

Raw and Juliano became the go-to text and teacher for this refined take on Wigmore's work; though she isn't mentioned anywhere in the book, her ideas are everywhere. In 2008, Laura Reiley of the *Tampa Bay Times* wrote of raw foods, "Somewhere between a religion and a culinary movement, the living-foods movement was inspired by Viktoras Kulvinskas and Ann Wigmore in the late 1960s, then glamorized by raw-food chef Juliano."[7] From the 1999 publication of *Raw*, raw food began its sexy moment, cutting itself off from the questionable origins of its godmother.

It would take a bit more culinary pedigree to really see the "living foods" movement taken seriously, and that would be provided by Charlie Trotter, the Chicago chef who had long provided vegetarian tasting menus to guests and wrote the vegetarian fine-dining book *Vegetables* in 1996. His longtime guests Michael and Roxanne Klein—he a tech entrepreneur, she a graduate of the California Culinary Academy—started to come to him asking for vegan meals, and he obliged. Then, after they met actor Woody Harrelson (he's a mainstay in the raw vegan circuit) on a culinary tour of Thailand, they tried out raw foods, and asked Trotter to see what he could do. The result was 2003's *Raw*, by Trotter and Roxanne Klein.

The change had been brewing before the book came out. In 2002, Kim Severson wrote in the *San Francisco Gate* of Klein's sixty-two seat eponymous restaurant Roxanne's, "In Roxanne's polished, subdued dining room, health food zealotry has no place. The emphasis is on flavor and service. It's the first raw-food restaurant for people with a palate who don't want to be punished for eating healthy."[8] This was the way people had responded to Deborah Madison and Greens in the '80s: finally, vegetarian food for *normal* people. The cookbook with culinary royalty followed, complete with recipes for things like "rawmesan" and a plain cashew cheese made with rejuvelac, a Wigmore invention. Again, she's not mentioned.

In the interview for that piece, Trotter told Severson that just as vegetarian food had become so commonplace that chefs at upscale restaurants needed to provide better options than simply removing the meat or fish from a plate, raw veganism would be just as normalized in five years' time. He wasn't right about that—it's such an expensive, time-consuming, and frankly monotonous way of eating that it would never get there—but the techniques and ingredients used have been deeply influential. Wigmore developed them initially, Juliano did a crude version, and Klein perfected them with culinary school know-how and taste. Trotter's imprimatur might have helped get coverage, but raw food still couldn't take off in the way they predicted. As Anthony Bourdain wrote in his 2006 book *The Nasty Bits*, he admired the concept, the challenge to do something new with gastronomy, but he couldn't get past the influence of Harrelson nor the picture of this rich American refusing to eat most of the food in Thailand. While Trotter, Klein, and Juliano truly believed that raw vegan food might be normalized over the next few years, Bourdain saw that future as a concern—not just because of his deep prejudice against vegetarians and vegans, but because it would further cut people off from the cuisines of the world. Just because an actor suggested it.

The book that Trotter and Klein came up with is a true triumph, with a cover image of bok choy with roots shot against a stark black background. All the things Wigmore and Brotman had wanted to do is done here, in a way that is refined, that doesn't scream at you about enzymes. Raw food built much of its reputation upon the promise of health and thinness, and those things only. By recognizing the potential of it as a technique-driven style of cooking, Trotter and Klein did create something of lasting influence, even as raw food is now seen as a total culinary anachronism, even among vegans.

Raw includes notes from both sommelier and farmer, to tie it into a serious chef lineage, and doesn't include pictures of the authors— this is about food, first and foremost. In the first recipe, for wakame sushi rolls, I notice a mention of a pine nut mayonnaise, the recipe for which can be found later in the book, and I remember finding out that one could make mayonnaise from nuts and what a revelation it was to me as a young vegan. Pine nuts are pricey, but so flavorful. They added the technique of smoking; finally, not everything was sprouted or soaked or spiked with rejuvelac. Here, there are black truffles, porcini mushrooms, an extravagant portobello mushroom pavé consisting of thin layers of marinated portobellos. There is luxury here and not just blenders and dehydrators, but a real understanding of flavor.

This is why Roxanne Klein could have, really, maybe, changed the game for raw food. But she and her husband, who was bankrolling her restaurant, got divorced in 2004, just one year after the book came out. (It seems they got remarried eventually, selling a $31 million San Francisco home in 2015.)[9] Though she had plans to get a grocery-store line of products out into the world, it didn't materialize.

The raw food craze spread, though, moving to the East Coast. Quintessence had opened in 1999 on East Tenth Street (again, Harrelson is mentioned in coverage as a fan) and Pure Food and Wine in 2004; both would close in the 2010s.[10] Pure Food and Wine put out a cookbook in 2005, called *Raw Food/Real World: 100 Recipes to Get the Glow*, authored by its cofounders, the couple Matthew Kenney and

Sarma Melngailis. Once again, raw food was less about the food and more about the feeling, the look one could achieve by consuming the right living enzymes. (In their book, Wigmore's work is mentioned as recommended reading.) "By eating raw foods, we build up our enzyme reserve," they write. They write about not having to scrub cooked grease from pots and pans anymore, imagining the same cooked grease sticking to their insides.

Kenney had been named a *Food & Wine* Best New Chef in 1994, having opened his namesake New York City restaurant, Matthew's, one year earlier. He went on to open a string of restaurants, until he tasted raw foods in the early 2000s. "I couldn't wait to crack into this mystery world and, even more importantly, to make my mark on it," he wrote in his 2015 memoir, *Cooked Raw: How One Celebrity Chef Risked Everything to Change the Way We Eat.*

Indeed, like Trotter, he took a precise technique to plant-based raw foods. But swiftly after the opening of Pure Food and Wine, Melngailis and investor Jeffrey Chodorow pushed him out. There was drama of such a high order that their breakup was covered on the *New York Post*'s "Page Six." When Pure Food and Wine closed for good in 2015, it was because Melngailis had disappeared with her husband, Anthony Strangis, after not paying employees. It was a Domino's pizza order made by Strangis in Tennessee that next year that blew their cover, and they were charged with stealing from investors, employees, and avoiding sales tax.[11] Melngailis spent time in jail at Rikers and has written of her regret on her blog, noting Strangis's emotional abuse; the trajectory and tragedy were sketched out more fully in the 2022 Netflix documentary *Bad Vegan.*

But the drama and the Domino's really put the kibosh on raw food as a cool moment in food—it wasn't the first gossip-page drama, as it followed the Kleins' divorce and the revelation that Quintessence's chef had been exposing himself to people on the subway. Kenney has continued to write raw foods cookbooks and has opened a slew of vegan restaurants around the world. Heirloom, which opened after he left Pure Food and Wine, notably served all its dishes vegetarian, vegan, and raw—an ambitious concept that couldn't last. His restaurant empire now has many restaurants with different cuisines (from pizza to burgers to a few plays on "farm to table") in cities across the world, from Bahrain, Baltimore, and Bogotá to Dubai, Los Angeles, and Providence, Rhode Island, site of a full vegan food hall called Plant City. His Food Future Institute is an online vegan culinary school (on its website, a raw zucchini lasagna is prominently displayed).

Kenney's continued success shows that raw foods, when the flavors and technique are integrated into a broader plant-based philosophy, serve a purpose. Were he teaching only raw food cooking and opening only raw food restaurants, I wouldn't be noticing that prominent chefs in Buenos Aires are visiting his new restaurants in Argentina. Despite how much raw foods owe to someone like Ann Wigmore, it's undeniable that their brief moment as the hot vegan thing made a lot of changes to how folks cook and think about plant-based foods. From the *Chronicle* giving stars to both Juliano's and Roxanne's restaurants to Trotter's involvement in a massive cookbook to Kenney being a Best New Chef who gave it all up for plants, this was a legitimizing moment. Perhaps it had to be so radical in order for vegan cuisine to get to a place where Dirt Candy became the first vegetarian restaurant to get two stars from the *Times* in seventeen years (Amanda Cohen, its chef-owner, worked at Kenney's Heirloom and opened Pure Food and Wine).

The relationship between veganism, vegetarianism, and a health ideology focused solely on the maintenance of an acceptable thin body is a real one, and this relationship hit a fevered pitch with the popularity of raw foods. To get people to give up on all the flavors and cooking techniques, as well as many vegetables, that they know and love, you have to promise them something great in return. What did raw foods promise? Freedom from disease. Beauty. Vitality. *A glow.* All of these are hard to resist. While counterculture, feminist, and punk approaches to meatless eating were all concerned about cultural norms and about eating in a way that would tread lightly on the world, raw foods—while at times a way of getting people to be less reliant upon Western medicine—were strictly utilitarian. Even at their most innovative or delicious, they were about the right enzymes, the right vitamins. And yet their culinary legacy is in fermented nut cheeses and decadent desserts.

Raw foods live on—undoubtedly, on a small scale—as a niche of veganism whose popularity is briefly renewed when another fad diet comes along, contorting itself to be gluten-free, paleo, keto, or plant-based—whatever the buyer wants. Few people could ever commit to it with enthusiasm, though folks like @fullyrawkristina on Instagram have one million followers looking for beet juice recipes to ensure a flat stomach. Is this a help or a hindrance to people giving up animal products generally? Where is the recognition of expense, of barriers to access that would keep people from consuming a sufficient number of calories on this diet?

Veganism's association with the hyper-restrictive raw foods movement has harmed its reputation; it has sometimes prevented it from being taken seriously, in many of the ways Wright outlined in her chapter "Death by Veganism." Food-wise, though, there were a few important things learned from this approach that continue to influence how vegans cook today: The focus on technique, on vegetables, fruits, and nuts without obsessing over protein or appealing to an omnivore's palate. That raw vegan food was full of invention and playfulness. These were crucial lessons for plant-based cuisine—especially in the realm of non-dairy dairy.

8. NON-DAIRY DAIRY

If there's one battle where plant-based agriculture has won over animal agriculture, it's the one regarding milk, and though non-dairy milk is a new fad in the US popular imagination, it's actually been around since at least 1226 CE. That's when almond milk was first mentioned in a manuscript by "the scribe of Baghdad," Al-Baghdadi, called *A Baghdad Cookery Book*. Soy milk, called *doufujiang*, is mentioned in *Remnant Notions from I Ya*, which dates to around 1365. From there, soy milk tended to steal the show globally, with rice milk emerging in the early twentieth century. As of 2022, oat milk is king, and at any trendy urban coffee shop, you can find someone ordering their latte with oat milk and their breakfast sandwich with cheese. Such is the breakdown of coherence when it comes to non-dairy dairy.

Non-milk milks, of course, are both easier to make and easier to sell than vegan cheese. It requires taking the legume, grain, or nut and blending it with water; that's how simple it is to make at home. Commercial plant milks come with preservatives, stabilizers, flavorings, and sweeteners, depending upon which one someone picks up. The plant-based milk market accounts for 10 percent of the total milk market in North America, with oat growing in popularity but soy still selling the most globally.[1] This is one change that people are eagerly willing to make in their diet. Beef's poor press for its greenhouse gas emissions is rivaled only by dairy, with dairy cattle coming in third in terms of food-related emissions.[2] It helps, too, that switching milks for coffee or cereal doesn't involve a drastic change, and it's estimated that 68 percent of the world has an issue absorbing lactose—why start the day with a stomachache if oat milk tastes just as good and is now just as accessible as dairy?[3]

Vegan cheese has always been the harder sell when it comes to non-dairy dairy, because it has taken decades—or centuries, depending upon how you look at it—to come to a place where people understand how to apply Western cheese techniques to plant-based milks in a way that becomes legible to a palate reared on melty, stretchy, gooey cheese.

The story of how we've come to a place where artisanal fermented nut cheeses are sold at Essex Market in New York City, and where Starbucks no longer charges for "alternative" milk, is indeed long—and endlessly fascinating. Li Yu-ying, a biologist and engineer, established the first soy dairy in Paris around 1908, where he'd moved from China, likely Beijing. While in Paris, he decided to study agronomy at Chesnoy School of Practical Agriculture, about sixty miles southwest of the French capital. In 1905, he presented his first paper on soy at the Second International Dairy Conference, pointing out that soy would be beneficial to public health and the diets of the poor in the Western world.

Yu-ying, an anarchist, had a marked interest—as have many who are invested in soy as an efficient and diverse protein source—in creating foods that would feed the global population. To this end, he created the Tofu Manufacturing Company in Paris, where many Chinese students would come to work. In a 1915 telegram he sent to a friend, he says that sales had increased from five hundred pieces of tofu per month to an average of ten thousand per month. He also developed fermented soy-based cheeses in flavors such as Parmesan, Camembert, Roquefort, and Gruyère, according to patents and documentation of the time. William Shurtleff, coauthor of *The Book of Tofu* and historian of soy foods, calls Yu-ying's book *Soya—Its Cultivation, Dietary, Therapeutic, Agricultural and Industrial Uses*, published in 1912, "one of the earliest, most important, influential, creative, interesting, and carefully researched books ever written about soybeans and soyfoods. Its bibliography on soy is larger than any published prior to that time."[4]

It's likely that the types of cheese he was making were different approaches to fermented tofu, a practice referenced in Chinese documents in 1610 and called "something like cheese" by Englishman Basil Hall after a dinner in Okinawa, showing that fermented bean curd was eaten in both China and Japan. Tofu-makers around the world, including at Wo Sing in San Francisco in the late 1800s, would produce it alongside fresh tofu. Yu-ying first referred to fermented tofu as "fermented cheese" in a British patent filed in 1919.

Though Yu-ying was doing fascinating work at the start of the twentieth century (work that would likely be lost to time were it not for Shurtleff's rigorous bibliographies), Western ideas about cheese would continue to be rooted in animal milk. Though recipes in books like *The Farm Vegetarian Cookbook* suggested the possibility of cheese-like substances flavored with nutritional yeast, these weren't going to win over anyone who likes more complex cheeses. For vegan cheeses to have their mainstream moment, there needed to be a figure like Miyoko Schinner, another California-born cook, who took ideas from raw vegans, such as Wigmore's rejuvelac and the method of soaking nuts, to bring a new approach to vegan dairy to the mainstream (or at least to the aisles of stores as ubiquitous in the US as Target and Trader Joe's).

Before Schinner's recipes and Miyoko's Creamery brand would usher in a new day, though, there were only extremely processed, flavored oils masquerading as cheese on most supermarket shelves. Like the American vegetarian recipes of the '70s that relied heavily on dairy and less on complexity, these were cheeses only someone truly dedicated to a cause could love. That's why a lot of vegans simply opted out of cheese.

When vegan cookbook author and restaurateur Isa Chandra Moskowitz (introduced in chapter 5) became a vegan, most of the vegan cheese she was able to find on store shelves was "really processed, really stiff, and not melty," she said. "I just tasted melted crayons."[5]

So, like many vegans, Moskowitz learned to live without the stuff. Even today, thirty-three years after she became a vegan, she isn't all that interested in trying to replicate it at her Modern Love restaurants. "We're doing it the lazy way, like most people, probably, if they want to do homemade," she admits of the vegan cheese on her menu. "We're using things that are already fermented and umami and, like, acidic and nuanced," such as miso, nutritional yeast, and lemon juice. Recipes on her website, ThePPK.com, and in her cookbooks are similar. I've made the chipotle mac and cheese so many times that I know the recipe by heart, and the "cheese" sauce made from cashews works on pasta as well as nachos. For a lot of home recipes, one doesn't have to do too much work beyond soaking nuts and putting them in a blender with flavorings. This, too, is part of raw veganism's legacy.

But for every vegan like Moskowitz who doesn't really miss cheese, there are plenty who do. Now, they have far more options. While the old-school melted-crayon stuff hasn't gone anywhere, you can also find soft and hard non-dairy cheeses, yogurt, and even butter. There are now entire stores devoted to vegan dairy, such as Riverdel, a New York City operation that boasts numerous varieties of plant-based cheese sold mainly by weight.

Although vegan cheese hasn't enjoyed the same explosive growth as plant-based burgers or non-dairy milk, it has still managed to gain respectable ground: according to a recent market research report, the global vegan cheese market was valued at just over $1 billion in 2019 and is expected to grow almost 13 percent in the next seven years.[6] Major food companies like General Mills have gotten in on the act, launching non-dairy versions of Yoplait's "Oui" French-style line and cow milk–free Häagen-Dazs, even as they continue to make traditional products.[7] Today, the non-dairy dairy market has expanded enough to entice almost anyone, vegan or not, who is taking a break from dairy. In the process, vegan cheese has undergone an unlikely evolution from punchline to something that sits comfortably, even unremarkably, on mainstream supermarket shelves.

When you tell someone you're vegan, one of the most common things you hear in response is, "I could never give up cheese." For me, it was easy: I'd never gotten too into fancy cheeses, and a life-long lactose intolerance meant that without dairy, I was also a lot less likely to need to run to the bathroom for an emergency (experiences that account for a shocking number of my childhood and adolescent memories). It never struck me as sad that I wouldn't sit around a robust cheese board, slicing off chunks of aged manchego to put on crackers with fig and nut cake. I was choosing a different way of life. I also think, now, that supporting small dairy cheesemakers as well as artisanal vegan cheesemakers isn't incoherent: they're different approaches to the same thing, which is the not-so-delicious-sounding concept of fermented milk.

The first and most obvious reason people find giving up cheese difficult is that it is widely considered one of the most delicious and versatile foods on the planet, something melty, gooey, and complex that is often served in a warm and comforting way, whether in a grilled cheese, on pizza, or in macaroni and cheese.

On top of that, there are also those who say that dairy cheese has truly addictive properties. It contains casein, a protein that releases casomorphins into the brain. Casomorphins, not incidentally, are opiates. When the US National Library of Medicine revealed this finding in a 2015 study, the food media churned out articles with headlines likening cheese to "crack," because this was before everyone generally agreed not to use that word to flippantly and insensitively refer to food.[8] The revelation gave cheese lovers a scientific explanation for their inability to resist the lure of fried mozzarella sticks and Sunday-football nachos. "You're now armed with the knowledge that it's not your fault if you struggle with excess cheese consumption," *Thrillist* remarked at the time. "You have a sickness."[9]

Along with the fiendish difficulty of approximating the possibly addictive pleasures of real cheese, there is the tricky job of reproducing the science that makes cheese *cheese* in all its creamy, crispy, gloriously pungent cheesiness. A fermented food of extraordinary complexity, its successful production is determined by a mind-boggling array of factors, from microbial activity to air temperature to what kind of grass a cow has been grazing.

The process of making dairy cheese begins by taking milk from an animal, heating it, and then acidifying it through the addition of cultures (or bacteria). A coagulant is typically added to turn the milk proteins into solid curds—in many cheeses, that coagulant is an enzyme called rennet, which is traditionally taken from an unweaned calf's stomach lining, although vegetarian rennet, derived from molds or plants, is used in some cases. After the milk curdles, its curds are separated from the whey to create a "mat" of curds that are cut and either salted or brined (depending on the kind of cheese being made), and then shaped and possibly aged.

Historically, vegan cheesemakers have not been able to come remotely close to creating products that mimic real cheese—no one was ever going to confuse rubbery, highly processed shreds of coconut oil and starch with mozzarella or cheddar. But that didn't stop them from trying, and over the last several years, their efforts have created a vegan cheese landscape that can be divided into three tiers, listed in ascending order according to quality, flavor, and texture.

At the bottom of the pile is the non-fermented oil-and-starch vegan cheese that you can find at most grocery stores—think Daiya's mozzarella shreds or Violife's aged cheddar slices. Made from a combination of fat, starch, and flavors that have been emulsified and solidified, it melts only reluctantly, with a telltale kind of sadness. (This is the "melted crayon" cheese that Moskowitz was referring to.)

Above that is cultured, or fermented, plant milk cheese, which is made by adding probiotics and enzymes to nut or oat milk in order to create curds and whey. This yields vegan cheese with some of the funky notes and textural complexity of traditional cheese; perhaps the best-known examples are made by Miyoko's Creamery, whose rounds of cultured cashew cheese helped to transform the vegan cheese market when they debuted in 2014.

Small-batch artisan vegan cheese, the kind that oozes, stinks, and blooms as convincingly as its dairy counterparts, constitutes the highest and most rarefied tier of vegan cheese. The process for making fermented vegan cheese, which is most nut-based cheese, is quite similar to that used to make dairy cheese. A nut is soaked and then blended with water to create a milk base, to which a culture is added. The cultured milk is left to ferment, forming a curd. After the curd is drained through a cheesecloth, it is molded into whatever shape the cheesemaker desires. Vegan cheese made this way will usually be rather soft, but further aging is possible. Thanks to an array of up-and-coming purveyors and a growing number of vegan cheese shops, artisan vegan cheese has become an emerging force in the last few years, though it is far from infiltrating the shelves of major grocery stores.

The three tiers of vegan cheese found in grocery stores are not necessarily in competition with one another, just as a vegetarian burger shop like Superiority Burger isn't working against an Impossible Burger or a Gardein patty from the grocery freezer aisle. Vegan cheese companies are producing options for distinct markets, whether they're a grocery-store chain or an artisanal cheese shop, and also for distinct uses: sometimes you want vegan cheese that melts in a scramble or grilled cheese sandwich; sometimes you want vegan cheese that looks pretty and can be eaten on a cracker. But given that vegan cheese is still very much a niche product—unlike plant-based burgers, which are marketed to meat eaters, it is peddled largely to a captive audience, namely vegans and the lactose intolerant—there is still plenty of confusion about what it is, or what it can be.

In the Western world, the quest to make non-dairy cheese reportedly began in 1896. According to William Shurtleff and Akiko Aoyagi's *History of Cheese, Cream Cheese and Sour Cream Alternatives (With or Without Soy) (1896–2013)*, that was the year Dr. John Harvey Kellogg, breakfast-cereal titan and Seventh-Day Adventist, invented

Nuttose, a cooked peanut product that was also used as a meat substitute, for his vegetarian health retreat.

From the early twentieth century onward, soy was used to make vegan cheese-type substances and cream cheese, the latter of which is still a fixture of bagel shops today. The first documented maker of commercial soy cheese was Yu-ying, the anarchist who started the world's first soy dairy.

During the 1930s, there was a spate of development in soy-based cream cheese alternatives. Much of it was driven by Seventh-Day Adventists, who between 1911 and 1970 made most of the commercial cheese alternatives available in the US. The 1970s saw the birth of the tofu cheesecake, one of the first of which debuted in 1971 at the New York macrobiotic restaurant Souen. These were and are often still sold in health food stores; the recipe from The Farm in their *Yay Soybeans!* booklet called for soy cheese, made from souring fresh soy milk in a way that is similar to how dairy milk becomes curdled. This would track with The Farm's early interest and research into soy and tempeh, which had them ahead of the curve on fermentation.

It wasn't until the mid-1980s that recognizable cheese alternatives began to emerge in the form of brands like Soyarella, Soya Kaas, and Soymage. As their names suggest, all of these cheeses were manufactured from soy protein. They represented the latest approach to the production of non-dairy cheese—one that not incidentally happened to use casein, that addictive and decidedly not vegan milk protein. This use of casein made many vegans suspicious, not just of vegan cheese brands but anything that could be considered "cheese-like." To this day, "casein-free" often appears prominently on vegan cheese labels and manufacturer websites.

While processed soy cheeses were beginning to appear on store shelves and in *Vegetarian Times* ads, the raw food movement was developing ways of fermenting nuts and seeds into cheese-like pastes and sauces. Raw foodists—who don't consume foods heated above 118 degrees Fahrenheit—used cultivated, sprouted grains to ferment nut milks, which often resulted in products with whipped textures and overly tart flavors. But the raw foodists did make two great steps forward for vegan cheese.

The first was eschewing soy for nut-based milks, something that opened up new possibilities for creating more cheese-like products; the nut used most often, both then and now, is the cashew, which offers both high fat content and a malleable flavor that was a significant improvement over the unmistakable bean taste of soy.

Although they never attained much popularity beyond raw food circles, these nut cheeses contained an obscure ingredient that would prove to be the raw foodists' second great contribution to the broader development of vegan cheese: rejuvelac.

Rejuvelac, the fermented wheat berry beverage developed by Wigmore that found new life in haute raw cuisine, was embraced as a base culture for fermentation by home cooks and would-be vegan cheese artisans alike—and, eventually, by companies that discovered that nut milks can function much like dairy when bacterial cultures are added to them, something that had huge implications for the future of cultured vegan cheese.

It is "still sort of the gateway" to vegan cheese-making, said Karen McAthy, the chef and founder of Blue Heron Creamery, a vegan cheese shop in Vancouver, British Columbia. "I thought it was significant in that it introduced the idea of using bacterial cultures to change one substance to another substance"—which, she explains, allowed vegan cheesemakers to more closely approximate the kinds of bacterial cultures used in dairy cheese.

The funky liquid's most noteworthy contribution to the vegan cheese world may have been as the origin point for Miyoko's Creamery, the biggest name in fermented vegan cheese today. Its founder, Miyoko Schinner, began experimenting with rejuvelac back in 2010, when she was searching for ways to develop nut-based cheeses that were more sophisticated than the spreads she had been making in her home kitchen. Using rejuvelac, she was able to create a fresh mozzarella style–cheese from soaked cashews, xanthan gum, and agar (a vegan gelatin), along with a "pub" cheddar that used brown miso, nutritional yeast, and dark beer for added flavor.

Schinner, who was born in Japan, had started developing her own recipes after going vegan in her twenties. All of that experimentation lit an entrepreneurial spark. "Well, if I'm going to invent these new foods," she recalls saying to herself, "then I might as well sell them too."

She made her initial foray into business in the 1980s while she was living in Tokyo, where she sold vegan pound cakes that she toted around in a backpack by subway. They were made using *okara*, a fibrous by-product of tofu production. There wasn't a market for vegan products—no one knew what they were, Schinner said, so she sold the treats as "an interesting new pound cake that was nutritious because it was made from okara."

In 1988, she opened Now & Zen, a San Francisco restaurant where she served what she calls "very rudimentary cheeses," such as the mozzarella she melted on top of seitan parmigiana. Some of them made their way into her first cookbook, 1991's *The Now and Zen Epicure*, whose recipes for sour cream, mayonnaise, and pumpkin mousse used cashews as a replacement for cow's milk.

Schinner eventually shuttered the restaurant to focus on running a company that manufactured vegan foods. When she closed the business in 2003, she attributed its demise to a lack of interest in vegan food.[10] But she didn't have the same problem when she launched Miyoko's Creamery eleven years later: sales quickly took off through natural grocers and vegan specialty stores. The company received $6 million in funding from outside investors within its first three years of business.

The reason for all of this enthusiasm? Schinner had managed to revolutionize vegan cheese. Although she had relied heavily upon rejuvelac in her 2012 book *Artisan Vegan Cheese*, she subsequently figured out how to produce vegan cheese using the same fermentation process used to produce dairy cheese and yogurt. Instead of cow's milk, she used a heavy cream made from either nuts or oats, and then inoculated it with lactic acid. From there, the bacteria took over, feeding off the sugars in the cream to produce various flavors.

The result was cheeses that were a world removed from the emulsified oil-and-starch products on the market. In the eyes of both weary vegans and the lactose intolerant, they were thrilling: here were wheels of cultured nut milk that looked indistinguishable from something you'd find on a cheese board, with a variety of flavors and textures to boot. Soon, Schinner had been dubbed the Queen of Vegan Cheese.[11]

Miyoko's Creamery expanded rapidly, despite some pitfalls in scaling up its product. "We went from a 40-pound batch [of cheese] to a 2,200-pound batch," Schinner said, "and we suffered initially trying to figure it all out. Some of the products suffered in quality. There were some other mishaps that took place as we transitioned. But even with industrial processing, you can put things in place that really drive that artisanal flavor."

Today, Schinner's wheels of cashew cheese can be found on the shelves of over twelve thousand stores across the US, including Whole Foods and Trader Joe's. During the last few years, the company has added cheese shreds and slices to its repertoire, along with butter, which inspired a proposed class-action lawsuit over the company's use of the term "butter" to describe a plant-based product (the lawsuit was eventually dismissed).[12]

When I asked her how she figured out that cashews were perhaps better for replacing dairy than soy, she can't recall the specific moment of discovery. It stands to reason that *Now and Zen Epicure* was a significant starting point for mainstreaming the idea, and vegan reliance on the nut only increased over the next few decades—to a troubling degree, because of concerns regarding the water requirements of cashew trees and the often deeply disturbing labor practices in cashew farming. In many of the growing regions, women are the primary workers removing the shell of the cashews, which contain a toxin that burns their fingers. Only 3 percent of cashews are fair trade, meaning 97 percent of cashews sold in the global market don't have any oversight.

Miyoko's company has made an effort to be transparent about where the cashews come from, putting a video on its website about their source in Vietnam, where only rainwater is used to grow the trees, the toxic outer shell is removed using a machine, and workers are guaranteed decent wages and conditions. They've also donated to local schools around the factory. This is an important start, but it also shows how important diversifying a vegan diet and a vegan style of creating dairy is: sunflower seeds, oats, and pumpkin seeds are starting to have a moment for creating similar products, as it becomes more and more obvious that being heavily reliant on any ingredient sourced solely in the Global South will lead to worker exploitation.

Until there is a major reckoning with the cashew, though, questions on sourcing must be asked.

Now that the field has proven to be of real market interest, as Miyoko's has grown, so has its biggest competitor: Kite Hill, a company cofounded in 2010 by chef Tal Ronnen, the traditional cheesemaker Monte Casino, and Pat Brown, who is best known as the founder of Impossible Foods. Kite Hill debuted in 2013, a year before Miyoko's Creamery did, launching at Whole Foods with almond milk–based cheese. A year later, it branched out into cream cheese and yogurt, then added stuffed ravioli and other ready-to-go items to its portfolio, which now also includes almond milk ricotta, sour cream, and ranch and French onion dips.

At the time Ronnen cofounded Kite Hill, he was the chef and founder of Crossroads Kitchen, a vegan restaurant in Los Angeles. "Plant-based food should be more accessible to everybody," he said of his reason for getting into the non-dairy dairy business. "And even though I could make a great meal at a fancy restaurant, it's not going to reach as many people."

Ronnen also knew firsthand how much room vegan cheese had for improvement. During a stint at the Wynn Las Vegas hotel in the 2010s, he had been tasked with creating vegan menus for each of the property's restaurants. One day, the executive chef asked him to bring some plant-based products to a team meeting. When one of the chefs spit out a "cheese" that was then one of the few options on the market, "it was a real eye-opening moment for me," Ronnen said. "I knew that I couldn't use something or serve something or even introduce it to other chefs if it wasn't as good as its [dairy] counterpart."

Since its launch, Kite Hill has expanded from Whole Foods to Target, Kroger, Safeway, and Meijer, and consistently received millions of dollars in funding: over the last seven years, the company has raised $75.5 million from investors, including 301 INC, General Mills' venture capital outfit. The investment from General Mills, which sells four brands of dairy yogurt, reflects a broader industry shift: as the alt-protein market continues to grow, major food companies are trying to get a piece of it by creating their own plant-based products. In 2019, the meat-processing giant Tyson Foods announced it was launching a new brand dedicated to plant-based meat alternatives; that same year, the yogurt maker Chobani rolled out a coconut-based non-dairy line.[13] And in 2020, Boursin, a dairy brand known for its packaged soft, flavored cheeses, launched a dairy-free spread.[14]

The potential of non-dairy dairy has also captured the attention of the tech world, just as plant-based burgers did. In 2019, a Bay Area–based company called Perfect Day arrived on the scene with a blueprint taken from the meatless burger crowd: to make non-dairy products for people who would never willingly give up dairy. But unlike their fake-meat counterparts, Perfect Day's promise is not ready-to-eat foods, but an ingredient that allows other companies to create them.

"We're making whey protein, which many people already are familiar with as the sort of white powder that comes from milk and is the best in class in terms of nutrition for muscle recovery and helps with stunted growth and malnutrition," said Perfect Day CEO and cofounder Ryan Pandya. "It's pretty much a drop-in replacement for what you used to be able to do with their ingredients. So if someone wants to formulate a vegan cheese using our protein, really all they have to do is buy it from us, mix it into something that is a white liquid with the right protein content, and then just go through a traditional dairy cheese-making process."

To produce its proprietary whey protein, Perfect Day has taken "the gene sequence that corresponds to milk protein from a cow and figured out a way to get that information into the microflora," which they are feeding in tanks, Pandya explains. The microflora produces Perfect Day's "flora-based" whey, which the FDA approved in the spring of 2020.[15]

What Perfect Day is doing isn't new, exactly: Pandya, who is vegan, points out that for a long time, dairy cheese wasn't even considered vegetarian because of its use of rennet. When vegetarian rennet was developed in the 1970s and commercialized in the 1980s, "it wasn't done for any profitability reason or consumer trend reason or anything to do with animal welfare," Pandya said. "It was just economics—like, it just made more sense to use the latest in fermentation and biotechnology to figure out a way to make that enzyme without the extraction from an animal. And now we're going to see that the exact same technology that's literally been in use for decades is now going to be able to make cheese vegan, too. And so it's less about making vegan cheese; it's more about making cheese vegan."

Perfect Day is focused on selling its whey protein to big producers in the non-dairy field; if its efforts are successful, the company might crack the code to scaling up fermentation for producers that are currently putting out "cheese-like" products such as Daiya. And if that happens, you might one day see more mass-produced vegan cheese whose flavor and texture can compete with not just Miyoko's, but actual dairy cheese.

Perfect Day's big promises and lack of transparency give me pause. What I've learned, in watching the culinary changes that vegan and vegetarian foods have undergone over the last half-century, is that innovation is driven by people who first have an interest in making really delicious food from whole ingredients, motivated by wanting to live in a way that treads more lightly on the planet and sees many fewer animals born into life in factory farms. There is already plenty of innovation pushing the vegan cheese market forward—it's just happening on a small scale.

Across the country and beyond, tiny operations like Dr. Cow, Rind, Vtopian, and Blue Heron Creamery are creating wildly inventive fermented cheese made from nuts, seeds, oats, and legumes. Some of them are taking a literal page from McAthy's *The Art of Plant-Based Cheesemaking: How to Craft Real, Cultured, Non-Dairy Cheese*, a 2017 book that builds upon Schinner's earlier vegan cheese books to provide a full guide to equipment, sanitation, and food safety, as well as instructions on aging and rind curing.

McAthy insists she comes to cheese-making from the vantage point of science, not a particular love of cheese, though she started her journey while she was the executive chef at Graze Food and Drink, a restaurant in Vancouver. The limitations of rejuvelac inspired her to research ways to bring traditional lactic acid fermentation to plant-based milks. Her book, which she calls a "living, breathing" document, guides the reader through various starters—rejuvelac, non-dairy kefir, probiotic capsules, and even sauerkraut brine—before providing instructions on quick, noncultured "cheezes" (as McAthy calls them), the creation of curd from various nuts, and some hard cheeses, all of which she breaks down in intense but accessible detail.

Given McAthy's expertise and scholarship on the subject, it's not surprising that Blue Heron has been producing the vegan cheese world's most dairy-esque products since 2016: its dried herb-powdered and wine-soaked rounds look nearly indistinguishable on a cheese board from dairy. But that's not actually McAthy's intention.

"My personal goal has always been that I really want to try to create or expand the boundaries of cheese-making, period," she said. "So that means I'm happy to use the analogous term that people have a reference point for"—some of her cheeses resemble blues and Camembert—"but I'm just trying to create new cheeses." This brings up the question of what cheese really is, exactly, and what vegan cheesemakers might be proving is that it's simply fermented milk. Could be cow's or goat's milk, or it could be cashew.

For Michaela Grob, the owner of Riverdel, the vegan cheese counter in New York City's Essex Market, the Blue Heron approach is what brings people to her business, where cheese is sold by weight and wrapped in traditional cheese paper. While most of the bigger vegan cheese producers can't have their products sold by weight because they're more interested in scaling up packaged products, "most of the small purveyors are actually very happy about it, because it's easier for them to make a five-pound wheel of cheese than packing it into 15 little packages," Grob said. "That's why we can work with people that are not even ready to do retail yet."

When Grob opened her original store in Brooklyn in 2015, she was stocking every available type of vegan cheese, from big brands like Daiya and Chao to tiny artisan operations like upstate New York's Cheezehound, which packaged its mozzarella in Mason jars. Because the market has expanded so much in the last five years, Grob now sees her role as pushing the smaller artisanal market with her own products and those of other makers, from Philadelphia's Bandit (formerly known as Conscious Cultures Creamery) to Portland's Vtopian.

But while people in the vegan cheese world know its diversity, plenty outside of it don't, and on a daily basis, Grob finds herself educating customers who want to broaden their non-dairy consumption but are overwhelmed not only by their choices, but also by the distinctions between cultured and non-cultured cheeses. "They don't know that there's so much out there," Grob said.

To compensate for this lack of familiarity, some larger vegan cheesemakers are educating consumers by selling their products to food-service companies, an approach that has proven lucrative for the makers of plant-based burgers and milks. Impossible Foods, for example, has collaborated on a breakfast sandwich with Starbucks, which has also reportedly been doing test runs of cream cheese from Miyoko's Creamery.[16] The chain began exploring more plant-based options after announcing that dairy products are its biggest source of carbon dioxide emissions.[17]

The food-service approach is one that has worked for NUMU, a New York–based company that makes mozzarella with coconut oil and non-GMO soybeans. Since launching in 2015, NUMU has sold its cheese only to restaurants, steadily increasing its presence on pizzas across the city, from pies at Lucali to Paulie Gee's Slice Shop to Scarr's. "We set out to really kind of infiltrate the non-vegan space. Our goal was to work primarily with non-vegan establishments," said NUMU cofounder Jill Carnegie of the company's strategy.

"We had more of an attitude of, we care about animal rights, and we care about the environment, and we hope that you care about those things too," Carnegie said. "But even if you don't, we know that you're going to love this product. So while we are unapologetically vegan, and we are unapologetically ethically motivated, our main goal is to keep it very social and friendly." At the end of 2019, the company was working with a co-producer to scale up its mozzarella recipe and continuing to focus on close relationships with restaurants instead of building its name on its own.

In early 2020, Miyoko's Creamery debuted more restaurant-ready products, including mozzarella shreds for pizzerias. "We are actively working with everything from burger chains to grilled-cheese restaurants to get these products out there," Schinner said. So far, their tests in these settings have gone well—meaning people were pleased with their products—and vindicated her belief that her non-dairy cheese is ready to compete with the big boys. When her new mozzarella was tested "at a major QSR [quick-service restaurant]," Schinner said, "a group of employees there had two pizzas side by side, their existing pizza with animal dairy and our pizza—they couldn't tell the difference."

There's little question that vegan cheese is ready to compete with dairy. The bigger question is whether the world is ready for it to. Despite all the faux-cheese shreds, slices, wheels, and spreads now available, most consumers, even the vegan-curious ones, have no idea what's out there. And so the true test of the industry's potential will be when more people do become aware of the options. Will the vegan cheese "ick" factor still be a deal-breaker when you can order a Little Caesars pizza topped with Miyoko's mozzarella and Beyond Meat sausage, when the bistro down the block has a non-dairy cheese platter on the menu alongside its traditional counterpart, when every hip restaurant in New York City offers NUMU and massive operations can do big-batch fermentation thanks to Perfect Day's animal-free whey?

The plant-based meat industry had been projected to grow in the coming years—that future is no longer so certain, following lagging sales in a post-pandemic world—but the fortunes of vegan cheese have always been less certain.[18] Pizza Hut will put Beyond Meat sausage on a pie, but to make it vegan, one needs to say "hold the cheese."[19] Will that soon change? As these plant-based meats take over market share at fast-food giants, we are certainly going to see vegan cheeses make their appearances as well. We're approaching a future where a late-night Domino's order could come complete with cashew-based mozzarella. Whether anyone will order it is one question that remains.

Another question is whether it matters, whether the success of non-dairy dairy can be measured by its availability at chain restaurants that otherwise don't care about how their ingredients are sourced or paying their workers a living wage. Vegan and vegetarian food-makers are held to a higher standard than omnivore ones—that's a fact, because by being dedicated to one particular facet of environmentalism and care, they are implicitly dedicated to more. What does it matter if the cashew cheese is vegan if the hands of a woman in India have been irreparably damaged by the nut shell's toxin? What does it matter if Oatly is in every coffee shop if one of its stakeholders is Blackstone, a private equity firm also invested in a company deforesting the Amazon and led by a CEO who donated $3 million to a super PAC supporting Trump's re-election?[20] More vegan food doesn't inevitably lead to a more just world, but it does let a lot of companies greenwash their money-making in its name.

Now that vegan and vegetarian food has become almost ubiquitous, now that more people understand its diversity and potential as
a way of being more environmentally friendly on a daily basis, the
movement must grapple with its future—and who owns it, who will
steer it. Historically, this has been the realm of counterculture folks—
hippies, anarchists, punks, chefs interested in alternatives to animal
agriculture. But the world of tech and venture capital is now sinking
its proprietary teeth in, and there hasn't been much of a fight against
this wave, which suggests the future of food isn't based on what grows
and what flows, but on what can be cultivated in a laboratory and
make a few people very rich, all under the guise of saving the planet.

9. THE FUTURE OF FOOD

As I write, I am looking at passion fruit in a bowl on my coffee table. A friend dropped them off because her tree was fruiting like mad; she couldn't eat enough of them to keep up, and she didn't want to let them rot. I had been stressed, and they're a natural blood pressure reducer. With a quarter of the bounty she gave me, I made a vegan panna cotta by mixing the fruit pulp with organic sugar, lime juice, and coconut milk over heat, all set with the littlest bit of agar powder I could get away with to ensure the texture was smooth but not gummy. Agar is a vegan gelatin made from seaweed, and too much of it makes a grainy texture. The panna cotta did what I think every good fruit dessert should do, which is make the passion fruit taste more like itself. Coconut milk mellows its natural tangy bite, while a small amount of sugar tempers its acidity. In a circular form, the end result is a bit retro, a bit '90s fine dining, but there's an undeniable elegance and timelessness, too. I'm so grateful for this fruit, for this line of creation and thought.

I served the panna cotta as dessert on Three Kings' Day, the twelfth day of Christmas, along with some vanilla shortbreads, some of which I dusted with hibiscus sugar I'd made. I gave my mother-in-law a bunch more to take home in a bag, and still I have many to eat myself. As with the banana blossoms I talked about at the very beginning of this book, the passion fruit were given to me freely, are the product of abundance and generosity, and were able to become so much more than what they seem to represent.

Sure, one still finds abundance in certain places—in San Juan, Puerto Rico, where I live, there is more fruit here than in other places—but there could be more fruit, more vegetables, more grains and legumes everywhere. The land, as Frances Moore Lappé has told us for fifty years, can provide. We just have a distribution problem, as well as an obsession with creating new things where the old could suffice. I write about food because I love to look at it, smell it, cook it, share it. I especially love to do these things with fruits and vegetables and beans—I love to show people what can be done, what's possible without involving animals for their flesh or their milk, their eggs.

Right now, I probably sound like one of the food writers I don't like, one of those food writers who turned a generation off ever thinking too deeply about what they ate, because then a box of Kraft mac and cheese for comfort after a long day would be a sacrilege. Those food writers, the dreadful ones, seem to think that going to pluck an apple from their orchard and cook eggs from their hens over a wood fire is a normal way of eating. Or is this just parody? I know I don't eat in a normal way, which is a product of a lot of luck and privilege, but that's why I want to advocate for a world where luck and privilege have no role in whether one's food is fresh, nutritious, culturally appropriate, and accessible. That's the future of food I want.

What's been strange as a food writer who has focused on meatless food is how, in the last five or so years, I have been distracted from the food that grows from the ground by products that promise innovation, that continue to hide the planet, to hide the joy of cooking—to indeed make, to use Carol J. Adams's concept of the absent referent, the earth itself the new absent referent. The animals might be absent in this idea of the future, industrial animal agriculture decimated by the dominance of tech burgers and lab meat, but meat as an idea will remain and it will continue to be the dominant food. There's been so much work done to change that idea, yet capital is leading us right back.

The only thing that has changed in the last few years is that tech meat such as Impossible Foods burgers and Beyond Meat burst onto the scene; now, lab meat is discussed as though inevitable, despite reporting that suggests it will never actually make it to market at a scale that will be affordable.[1] Suddenly, despite my commitment to vegetables, I was tasked with untangling what meat facsimiles mean. But I don't eat these products, and I don't actually care about them beyond what they represent. What they represent is a continuation of meat-as-symbol that I find rather troubling, because I personally want to see a radical reimagining of how we eat, how we use land, and how we think about our food.

Yet this is what is being called "the future of food." I've experienced this shift myself, all the while rejecting and questioning it—while continuing to pursue the joy of sharing vegetables and fruits, abundant as they are in Puerto Rico.

It all happened suddenly at the magazine where I was working in New York City. Though this small, local publication had made its name focusing on urban rooftop farms and craft beer, we were eventually tasked with covering "tech"—food tech. This meant everything from vertical indoor farming to 3D-printed cookies. The common denominator was always a lot of money, usually supplied by venture capital. These weren't the small pierogi shops that most readers were on the lookout for; these were mainly male-staffed start-up operations looking to "innovate in the food space," to use their parlance. Basically, they wanted to fix something (the global food system) that had been broken by capitalism with more, better capitalism. They saw that the world needed saving, and they figured they could make money while pretending to save it.

One evening I was sent to check out an event held in a fake apartment, where a chef I knew mainly from him yelling about the inedibility of raw red onions on the Food Network show *Chopped* would be using a fancy new oven to make passed appetizers for the media crowd. (I had agreed with him about the onions, but I don't remember whether they were served on anything that I actually ate.)

The cofounder of this oven operation showed us how it worked, reminding me a lot of the guy showing off a primitive computer in *Willy Wonka* who promises it can predict the location of the Golden Tickets (it cannot). With this oven, they told us, you could cook using your iPhone. No more worrying! It would program everything and you could look on from the couch in the other room, or even as you walked back from the subway.

An older woman in the crowd raised her hand to ask what was a genius question under the circumstances: "Would it be better to bake a pie in a glass or metal plate in this oven?" The cofounder said he'd have to check on that; he wasn't sure. The question was genius because it pulled the curtain back and revealed the wizard was actually just a man pushing levers and pressing buttons: this was an oven made by people who don't care much about food, and don't expect anyone else wants to cook either. They were attempting to solve a problem that they created. No one asked for this. The ovens I still see in the kitchens of food people, through their Instagrams, have gas ranges or induction burners. They're not interested in cooking via iPhone, in being distanced from their senses. Our human senses are the very basis of cooking: at the very least, even for the very worst cook, innate knowledge is what keeps us from burning everything we put in a pan to a crisp.

A few years later on, after being fired and re-hired by this very magazine (only to be fired again, or, to put it more gently, "laid off for budgetary reasons"), I went with the publisher to check out some other operation that was being housed in its investors' Columbus Circle office for the time being. They were 3D-printing food—recipes and ingredients were put into the machine, then spat back out in the desired formation. Perhaps a flower; maybe the outline of an elephant. What was the technology's use? They said something about making it easier for people with swallowing issues to eat, which is a noble pursuit, but they were also trying to sell their presence in Michelin-caliber restaurant kitchens, where pastry chefs wouldn't, say, have to pipe a chocolate design over and over again. It would be uniform on every plate. Why would this be preferable to the studied human hand, the beauty of slight differences? Because efficiency is the only language tech and business people know.

These two inventions seemed dead in the water to me (maybe they're not—I don't care to look them up), yet they're useful anecdotally to explain why I am pessimistic about "food tech": it's not about providing real solutions; it's about money, and the people making the money don't really care how people eat or cook or why people love food. For this reason, I'm dubious of invention, of "innovation." I'm what you might call a "techno-pessimist"—someone who doesn't believe the fixes we need for the planet, animals, and human beings are going to be found by creating something proprietary and new, something that will be owned. (I always envision a dystopian time in which a vertical urban farm run by a benevolent-looking tech bro sells us subscriptions to lettuce, the way we pay for Spotify; we will also be able to tack on a lab meat subscription from their partner company, I'm sure.)

We know what the planet needs, and it's the radical restructuring of land use—this is what the United Nations Intergovernmental Panel on Climate Change has told us. We know what the people need, which is self-determination with regard to farming for the Global South, as well as for the Black and Indigenous people upon whose land the United States and other nations settled. Indigenous farming practices and agroecology are the documented ways forward, as well as a new economic system that isn't built upon cancerous, endless growth. Instead, we're getting steaks made in a lab. Who asked for this?

I suppose it doesn't matter who asked for this, when the media and many others are lapping up stories of new green tech that promises to solve the problem whose cause is ultimately an obsession with consumption, and a manufactured lack of self- and community reliance in "developed" countries. It will never cease to shock me that people would rather spend millions creating "meat" out of all sorts of products than simply stop eating meat or make meat a treat.

It's this capitulation to endless consumption that makes all this stuff problematic. Because that's what it is: stuff to buy. There's nothing necessary about any of it.

There has been growing pushback to the notion that the only way forward is to hand the keys to the food system over to people who would like to remake it in the image of technology, even if doing so leads to being called a "foodie," an "aesthete," or a "Luddite" by those who believe in this vision of the future. Journalist Charlie Mitchell wrote a piece for *The Baffler* called "Fake Meat, Real Profits" in 2021 that argues tech meats are not saving the planet; they're only getting their producers rich. Cheekily, he said:

> The archetypal alt-meat hero is a white man with a graduate degree who played college football. When his journey begins, he's bored in a cushy corporate post, secure in everything except his ego. All the good that he hoped to do—Eat Just cofounder Josh Tetrick joined humanitarian projects in sub-Saharan Africa, Beyond Meat founder Ethan Brown worked in renewable energy—it's not happening fast enough. Our hero has an incredible idea, calls a friend about it, that friend calls a venture capitalist, and soon, the man presides over a glitzy headquarters, surrounded by scuttling scientists and Michelin star chefs, serving reporters and investors with small-plate samples, spinning yarns and making bold predictions.[2]

Michele Simon, JD, MPH, established the Plant Based Foods Association in 2015 after going vegan in the late '90s and finding the movement to be "apolitical" and "potluck-focused." With PBFA, she wanted to provide support to companies creating products that help people move from an animal-centered diet to a plant-centered one. The strategy was to push for policy changes that would create a new food environment in which it would be easier for people to eat healthier. Products from tech meat companies like Impossible Foods or Beyond Meat were part of that vision. She left PBFA in 2020. As someone who's attempted to make plant-based foods part of a bigger food movement, one geared toward sustainability broadly speaking, she now spends her time writing and talking about the real impact of plant-based foods, an honesty that is refreshing and often lacking. In a piece for *VegNews*, she showed that tech meats aren't making a real dent in how much meat people are eating, and when I talked to her on the phone about her career, she told me that it would behoove the plant-based foods movement to be honest about how small and niche it is.[3]

Honesty is her strong suit as a voice in this space. One especially telling and biting piece by Simon was for *Forbes*, about how lab meat advocates can learn from the conviction of Theranos founder Elizabeth Holmes, who was found to have defrauded investors because of her fabrications and lack of scientific understanding. Simon compares the big claims, promises, and celebrity ties of Holmes to those of the lab meat industry, providing a biting critique of the way venture capital is set up to reward concepts that *sound* good but aren't grounded in reality. Especially important is her observation that these companies won't be able to get away with calling their technology "proprietary," because people want transparency about what they eat.[4] Consistently, the food tech boosters take for granted the idea that people do not care about what their food is made of, and how and where it's made, banking on the continued disinterest of Americans in their food's origins.

Outside the US, there's more incredulity in general around the idea that these companies can "fix" climate change, as many folks in the Global South have already seen what happens when the West "invests"—or rather, intervenes—in traditional food. I called up Andrea Hernández, the Honduras-based writer and marketing expert behind SnaxShot. I wanted to know what it's like to write on the subject of branding in food and beverage, as well as many of the options that purport to "fix" the world such as "plant-based" meat, from the perspective of someone who doesn't have access to these things where she lives. Hernández told me that while she can't pick up an adaptogen-laced seltzer, she has ancestral knowledge of various herbal remedies and access to fruit carts on every corner where she can get the remedies' ingredients from local growers. That seems ideal, no? Like something we all should have!

As we talked, we focused a lot on how the United States, as a settler state, destroyed ancestral knowledge of the land and the medicinal purposes of what it could grow, and so as an imperialist and capitalist entity, its corporate arms go around the world to extract resources to sell back to its people. One example Hernández mentioned was the newfound popularity of hibiscus as a flavor. Many people she was speaking to first tried it in a beverage at Starbucks, despite the fact that *agua de Jamaica* already exists as a traditional and cheap drink to make.

Corporations also always try to expand their markets where there is already tradition and history. See: Impossible Foods, Beyond Meat, and Eat Just—all makers of plant-based or "tech" meat—trying desperately to get into the market in Asia, a continent of many nations that have plant protein traditions. They would no doubt like to kill those traditions and create a reliance on their products.

That's the kind of situation that is happening in Ethiopia, where Britt H. Young reported for *N+1* on the replacement of traditionally consumed local chickens by a hybrid meant to encourage Ethiopian people—who rely more on beef—to switch to chicken for its more climate-friendly reputation. Young defines a resilient chicken as one that allows farmers to no longer need the state: "In this new era of climate adaptation development, the desired outcome is to discipline a neoliberal subjectivity comprised of subsistence farmers who internalize the state's neglect of them."[5]

The thing is, this chicken tastes bad. It doesn't hold up to traditional preparation. So what's its value? It's as a commodity that greenwashes reality, though we already know this kind of effort doesn't work. I called Young up to further discuss her piece, and she told me that the idea of the market as the only entity that has the means of stemming climate change is, from her research, globally pervasive.

In *Eating Tomorrow: Agribusiness, Family Farmers, and the Battle for the Future of Food*, Timothy A. Wise writes of a similar project in Malawi, where "high-yield" seeds developed by scientists in the Global North replaced heirloom seeds.[6] The yields declined year after year, requiring farmers who usually save seeds and share them with neighbors to buy new ones as a matter of course. Local women call the hybrid version of maize "a marriage breaker" because it doesn't make a good enough dish for their husbands; local varieties are "marriage builders." It's the rules attached to those subsidies (e.g., use GMO seeds, not heirloom) that force farmers' hands into what isn't traditional, into an arrangement that requires constant purchasing. Whose brilliant, climate change–resilient future is this?

In February 2021, Bill Gates gave an interview to Kara Swisher at the *New York Times* where he discussed "flying around Africa" and "seeing, you know, no electricity and wondering, how do we electrify all of Africa?" This has a big, stinky whiff of "Do They Know It's Christmas?"–type imperialist paternalism, and nowhere in this interview do I see Gates really interrogate his role as a male billionaire from the US; nowhere do I see him thinking about how to give the reins over to African people to lead their own forays into green energy, into regenerative agriculture and agroecology. (He also said, "It's important to say that what Elon did with Tesla is one of the greatest contributions to climate change anyone's ever made"—this is a car for individuals; the cheapest model goes for $46,990. Does Bill Gates think a banana costs $10, to paraphrase the famous *Arrested Development* meme?)[7]

These are the people with resources, with capital, and this is how they think: they don't ask the people what they need; they just make something that seems like a solution and say, "Ta-da!" The future doesn't need their visions; the future needs justice, reparations, the redistribution of wealth, and radical restructuring of who has land, who farms, and how land is used. Look at Texas, where in February 2021, three severe winter storms caused a power outage. The people suffered storms that the deregulated energy grid wasn't prepared for, and some natural gas suppliers, pipeline companies, and banks that trade commodities made billions of dollars.[8]

If this can happen in Texas, it doesn't really seem like people interested in new climate change "solutions" are doing a very good job. No one without water or heat is asking for a cow-free steak or a 3D-printed meal. What did help in that situation is the same thing that's always helped when the state is a failure: human beings providing mutual aid.[9] This is similar to Puerto Rico asking for food and water after Hurricane Maria; it's what people have needed in the COVID-19 pandemic, while suffering abandonment from governments, local and federal. Community fridges and the distribution of free meals have been a way of performing solidarity, as well as maintaining survival.

That effective responses to crisis largely happen on a small and local scale should be heartening. Karen Washington has famously been an advocate for better food policy in the Bronx, working from a foundation in community gardens. As Ligaya Mishan wrote in a deep piece on food activism in *T: The New York Times Style Magazine*: "She has since cultivated many gardens and drafted policy proposals for government officials, but the heart of her work is still local, done in and for her community."[10]

The community-level approach is one where every voice can be heard. "Equity is as important as technology," as Congressperson Alexandria Ocasio-Cortez has said.[11] The future doesn't need to be neo-colonized into the Global North's visions of "efficiency." We have to change how we live, how we engage with each other, who has power. Can we start to discuss justice-oriented food initiatives with the same breathless fervor with which we cover every capital-driven "innovation," as Mishan has done? Because the people don't need to cook with their iPhones. The people, everywhere, simply need power.

At the same time, we also need to change what we eat. But I understand why meat is the central idea in Americans' heads when it comes to gustatory pleasure: it's how most of us were raised. Someone posts a picture of fried chicken to their Instagram story and I remember everything about the taste of fried chicken—the salt, the pepper, the crack of skin giving way to moist flesh. I haven't eaten a piece of fried chicken in a decade, but the sense memory remains. Will I ever forget? Would it mean something to forget?

This happens a lot: someone posts prosciutto and I remember the wheels of it with mozzarella my mom would get at Costco that I would basically eat all by myself, repeatedly slinking to the kitchen to slice off just one more piece. Someone posts arroz con pollo and my mouth fills with the essence of *sazón*, a burst of pea. Someone posts a barbecue pork rib and I recall the sweetness and smoke, the slick of fat, my teeth touching bone. I know what all of it tastes like; I remember it vividly. Meat was at the center of my plate growing up. It nourished me; I took so much pleasure in it.

I remember these foods and I do what I was taught in meditation classes: see the thought, honor it, and let it go. There is nothing that could ever make me eat a piece of meat again, save for some hypothetical situation where I was stranded and starving. The mere thought of putting a piece of meat into my mouth makes me gag. I honestly do not know how most people do it, how they "meatpost," to use climate writer Emily Atkin's parlance, and meat-eat with abandon.

I don't doubt that many people are quite intentional about their meat consumption, but that's not the vision one gets online, and it occasionally drives me to climate despair. What would convince people to be more open to eating more vegetarian meals, more vegan meals? Why is being nonchalant about eating meat still so broadly accepted, especially in the food world? What would convince food writers and influencers to sometimes suggest it's okay not to eat meat at every meal? What would cause there to be good vegetarian and vegan options at hip restaurants? How do we adjust the narrative on what food is essential to eat, taking into consideration ecology, labor, welfare?

It's wild to watch the ideas contained in various texts on meat's meaning play out time and time again on the internet as well as in real-life conversation, because they've been inside my head for so long. I look on in a bit of awe, as well as a bit of annoyance: Of course abundant cheap meat represents masculinity. Of course abundant cheap meat represents the metaphorical virility and strength of the United States. Of course abundant cheap meat represents affluence. Of course a bunch of people believe President Biden is going to dictate they only eat four pounds of beef per year and will show off their poorly cooked steaks in protest. We know all of this.

To me, every kerfuffle about meat on social media brings with it a wave of the obvious and depressing. The US government subsidizes the industrial meat and dairy industries for $38 billion per year; meat and dairy are socialized food industries with horrifying working conditions in a country that won't give us Medicare for All or wipe away our student loan debt. Biden began 2022 by injecting $1 billion into meat processing to stir up "competition," when what is needed is less meat.[12] When will $1 billion be injected into small agroecological farms?

Meat maintains its central role because people can't imagine another way forward. Despite the strides documented in earlier chapters toward a vegetarian and vegan cuisine that can be enjoyed by all, omnivores seem to be under the impression that everyone who's chosen not to eat meat for ethical or spiritual reasons is happy to eat anything offered to them, so long as it has no animal products. How does this perspective persist in 2022, when it's been proven time and again that vegetarian and vegan food can be really good and really innovative? Why is the ascetic vegetarian or vegan still a stereotype? I've happily eaten a plain roasted sweet potato on Thanksgiving, of course, like any meat-eschewing person born into the settler-colonial United States, but that doesn't mean I want the barest plate imaginable every day of my life.

This feels absurd to even make these points here, considering all I've shared up to this point about bold and exciting plant-based cuisine, and I hope that if you're an omnivore reading this, you understand that even ethical vegetarians and vegans like to enjoy really delicious, well-seasoned food. I don't know if Pete Wells of the *New*

York Times is aware of this, though, because he published the following line in his takedown of Eleven Madison Park after its conversion to a "plant-based" menu: "Diners who don't eat animals for religious or moral reasons will probably welcome the new menu."[13] An odd assumption, Mr. Wells. (I hadn't been to EMP when it was omnivorous and haven't been there since it changed; the reviews and conversation around it are fascinating, however.)

Such assumptions suggest that there is no overlap in people's reasons for not eating meat, but one can have concerns about animal rights while still wanting to enjoy a really good meal. And while I, in typical vegetarian fashion, would say there is no such thing as humane slaughter, I also know—as I've written before—that the conscientious omnivore is our best ally in destroying industrial animal farming (though not in destroying tech meat, certainly not lab meat). So which is actually "better": EMP doing, by all accounts (public ones and private ones I've been lucky enough to receive), bad vegan fine dining, or returning to a style of food that includes slaughter but also supports a ton of local farmers? I don't want any animals to die for my food, but I know which is actually a better choice—environmentally, economically, and in terms of cultural influence.

My perspective doesn't make me popular with vegans. For one, I'm an ex-vegan. I had started to have questions months before I actually gave up veganism after five years by eating oysters in a grief fog. Veganism simply didn't feel reasonable to me anymore; I didn't understand how it could truly support local ecosystems and economies in the way that I had hoped it would, that I thought was right for the future. The more I learned about agriculture, the more I understood animals' significant role in it—the importance of working with them, toward common stewardship of the land.

I still find any condescending attitude toward animals' sentience, intelligence, and personalities appalling. Being a locally minded vegetarian has been my compromise. I'm sure that to many this is intellectually incoherent, to which I'd offer that it's not a purely intellectual choice. It's not pure feeling, either, though, as many want to suggest.

It's complicated, and it would be nice to see more omnivores capable of acknowledging that.

I've been challenged lately by my being in the Caribbean, where the lionfish is an invasive species. My husband and I saw signs warning of their stings while we were on Culebra, a small island in the Puerto Rican archipelago. According to a video from National Geographic, they arrived from their native habitat in the Indo-Pacific to somewhere north of Miami in the mid-1980s and now wreak havoc on local waterways. Without a native predator in the Gulf of Mexico and the Caribbean, they gobble up everything in sight, including tiny reef fish who serve important ecological purposes, such as excreting ammonium through their gills, which is essential for coral reef growth. Their disappearance is thus destroying reefs. As researcher Eric Johnson, a University of North Florida biologist, says, the best thing to do is to eat them—to create demand in supermarkets and at restaurants for this species, which provides ample work to local fishermen and can mitigate the lionfishes' impact on the ecosystem.

The issue of an invasive species is separate from real and big concerns around sustainable seafood. To understand the distinctions better, I talked to Jack Whalen, a sociologist and ethnographer who spent over a decade working with sustainable fisheries, to get an overview on the big issues. What he explained to me is that it's about the method of fishing, whether it's industrial or small-scale, because in the former, there will be overfishing—so that the population doesn't reproduce naturally and sufficiently—as well as other marine life getting caught up. Lionfish are caught by the small-scale method of divers using spears.

"If you just want to use [industrial technology] without much real thinking about what the consequences are going to be other than short-term profitability, you can harvest a lot of fish but way more than the fishery can sustain in terms of its maximum sustainable yield," Whalen told me in a 2021 interview. That yield "would be how much can you catch with not just the stock that you're fishing but the whole ecology there; that what lives there and breeds is maintained—not just survives, but continues to be healthy." To make sure seafood has been sustainably farmed, he recommends Seafood Watch.

Recently, at a restaurant in San Juan, we were told they had lionfish ceviche on the menu and were specifically made aware of its status as an invasive species, and why it would be important to eat it. I told the server that yes, I would eat this, but my husband is allergic to fish. I felt virtuous in this moment, for some stupid reason, believing that I would put aside my spiritual qualms—because that's what they are—about eating something with eyeballs that had once been alive, in order to eat a ceviche to, like, save the reef. What a martyr! I eat oysters because they don't have a nervous system and perform a critical ecological function, so eating them encourages demand. As many have said, they're basically meat plants of the sea: wouldn't eating lionfish be basically the same, aside from the presence of the nervous system, given the significance of their detrimental effects on the reef and native fish habitat?

Later our friends arrived and ordered the ceviche, and I was actually faced with this task: I did not want to do it, yet I had made this claim—I wanted to believe that when push really came to shove, I would put the environment ahead of my vegetarianism. From all that I've read, eating this fish is the only way to curb its population. Pushing its consumption is a really significant gastronomic act. One concern was rational, urgent; the other, emotional.

I ate a little piece, felt sad in the soul, and simply slurped up a bit of the *leche de tigre*. I want to accommodate the world; I want to actively eat what needs to be eaten to maintain equilibrium in the ocean . . . but it's strange and hard to do so after years without. I still feel very strongly that it's violent, while understanding why others would not feel that way. I understood why I rationally thought it made sense to eat the fish; I still could not eat it. "You can eat a whole piece," my friend said, with a light tone of mockery. "I can't," I replied, frowning at my plate, then mumbling, "It was alive."

But lionfish can also be part of a sustainable and apparently delicious diet. Dr. Hari Pulapaka is both a math professor at Stetson

University, a chef, and a cookbook author who only recently stepped away from the DeLand, Florida, restaurant Cress that he and his wife opened in 2008. He began serving lionfish in 2013 as part of "lesser seafood" dinners, trying to get diners to eat sustainable but under-consumed types of fish. His suppliers brought the lionfish to his attention, and he's used it in tacos, as a whole fried fish, in ceviche, and even as a lionfish bhel puri at the 2018 James Beard Awards.

"If anyone is even remotely interested in being a little bit more thoughtful about the food that they eat—leaving the vegetarian and vegan part aside—lionfish is really a great option, and they should support the divers who are working really hard to get this for the marketplace," Pulapaka told me over the phone in 2021. "And then understand that from the gastronomic point of view it is absolutely delicious. It's sweet, it's a mild-flavored white fish, semi-firm in texture, so it really doesn't look like a lot when you look at a filet of lionfish—it looks rather thin and flimsy, even less so than a flounder, actually. But when you cook it, it's really chef friendly, it's home cook friendly, and it tastes really unique and different because it's not like another fish. It actually has a distinctive flavor."

People are always bringing up different scenarios for me that they think might justify me eating a pork chop or a steak, and I try telling them that I don't see meat as food anymore. You certainly couldn't get me to eat a pig just because it was invasive, eating up everything in its path—even if this makes me a bad environmentalist. Theoretically, I would want to, I guess, just like the lionfish. But I wouldn't be able to. This is simply where my brain can't beat my heart. To get me to eat meat, or even a lionfish, you'd have to force-feed it to me through my tears and gritted teeth. I don't know if I can change at this point, though I have found evidence of at least one vegan who eats lionfish for the sake of the environment, and for others, this has been a really significant moral qualm and topic of conversation in various forums. Maybe I'll get over it—that's a possibility.

It is interesting, as I write this, to think that Saint Francis of Assisi (an icon of mine) is patron saint of both the environment and animals, supposedly advocating for both, because it brings us right to the lionfish question: What happens when one concern gets in the way of the other? When an animal is destroying the environment?

Well, we blame the humans, because it's their fault this invasive species is even in the wrong ocean on the other side of the world (how that happened is still debated). And then, I suppose, the conscientious omnivores eat up as much lionfish as they can: their own portion, and another for the vegans and vegetarians who do their part in other ways, every day, because the habitable future of the planet is going to require all of us working together. It's also going to require that the food taste good for everyone, because having an ethical or spiritual issue with eating animals shouldn't mean a life of beets that taste like lemon Pledge, regardless of what our most prominent restaurant critic might think.

When Epicurious announced that it is officially no longer publishing recipes that involve beef in 2021, a lot of people started to yell about how they should actually promote "sustainable" beef, despite the fact that there is no earth-friendly level or type of beef production that would be able to feed people the amount of beef they're accustomed to eating. Something has to give. Consumption must decrease.

It's also true that dairy, shrimp, chicken, and other livestock also have awful impacts on the environment in addition to being industries with abysmal animal welfare and human labor conditions. There needs to be more nuance in the conversation.

But food media at large does not take climate change seriously. Not really. I'm talking about the major magazines and food sections, which take no stands at all on sourcing, and don't do much to educate readers on the food system's massive greenhouse gas emissions. That would just be too much of a bummer! This move by Epicurious is something, and it is bold, and I hope the conversation they've begun broadens and deepens into the rest of the issues with the food system beyond beef. At least they're saying something, anything.

Meat also stays central because the way we talk about vegetables often mimics how we speak about animal carcasses and flesh. Or

perhaps I'm speaking only for myself. Despite my belief in the supremacy of vegetables, fruits, legumes, and grains, my language of cooking
is decidedly meat-centric. I butcher jackfruit and panapén. I cut kale
off its ribs and save the bones. I scoop out the eggplant's innards. I
stuff the hollowed-out cavity of a squash. I peel off the skin of onions
and think about how in Spanish there are different words for the skins
of vegetables and animals: *Cáscara. Cuero.* A clove of garlic, though, is
a *diente*, a tooth. Our bodies are the map of our gastronomy, whether
human or non-human animal.

I became obsessed with writing an essay about bones in 2018,
which was years after bone broth (a bit of a misnomer) had debuted
on the New York scene with Marco Canora's Brodo. What was going
to be my way into bones, as a vegetarian? How would I write about
bones without making it read like vegan propaganda? I just wanted
to think through what it means for an animal's very bones to create
so much of the basis of gastronomy. From what I've read, learning
to make stock is one of the first lessons in culinary school. I wanted
to ponder the inclination to suck out bone marrow, something I'm
told my grandmother loved to do. Marrow bones on a plate were
cool (they're still cool—I saw one on Instagram last week), because
insouciance is cool, and what's more insouciant than eating the inside
of literal bones?

In 2016, I broke two bones in my foot walking down the stairs
of my Crown Heights apartment building. The experience made me
think about the meaning of bones, their essential functions. Breaking
bones reminded me that I had bones to begin with. It made me think
about the omnivore's act of putting a chicken's carcass stripped of flesh
in a pot of water and boiling it, until all flavor had been extruded—until there was a thick liquid left behind that would allow the animal to
live on, night after night, until exhausted through risottos and soups.
What we leave behind on this planet once humanity is exhausted will
be chicken bones. They litter the streets, too, which I only discovered
after I got a dog. Chicken bones are everywhere, posing a danger to
Benny's health and building our legacy: a legacy of modification and

industrialization and confinement of animals. What has given us this measure of abundance has been a political and ethical failure, the cost of which is potentially our very existence.

Whenever I talk to conscientious meat-eaters, they tell me about how they use up every last bit of the humanely raised animals they purchase and eat. Because I think of things differently after a decade of not seeing animals as food, I wince a bit: I think about my bones being boiled, my fat being stored in a jar for later. This is why no one wants a vegetarian to write about bones: we sound hysterical. And because the future probably doesn't involve everyone giving up meat completely (though perhaps bit by bit, it will happen, if new California animal welfare regulations are a bellwether), it's probably best to listen to the conscientious omnivores. I'd prefer to live in their world than a corporate processed-protein dystopia, even if I continue to abstain.

But the world of the conscientious omnivore and happy vegetarian living in harmony is no longer presented as an option. It's an anachronism, apparently. Now we have two perspectives on the future being presented to us: continue with factory farming and monocropped GMO corn and soy, or surrender to the world of tech meat where we replace those with pea and oat. The "meatless future" envisioned at *Vox* is one that doesn't even consider the potential of supporting small farmers, of supporting agroecology, or of the universal basic income and guaranteed housing and free college tuition and nationalized health care that would create conditions for people to cook and even grow their own food. It's just the same shit, removing the animals. It's displacement of the problems when what we need is far more radical.

The lab meat being developed for possible future consumption doesn't have bones. Lab wings would be boneless; lab ribs—how would those work? There wouldn't be meat stock, gelatinous and thick. It's funny to me, of course, that the development of these products wouldn't (or rather, couldn't) take into account this gastronomically significant aspect of eating animals, one that conscientious meat-eaters are so attached to—would lab meat have fat drippings?

With these products, meat would be only its essence. It would perform no other function but its most base one. I know that these products are only about replacing the cheapest, most broadly consumed meat, which means it is a nutritional experiment for the poorest folks while the rich continue to suck on elegant marrow bones, to have a quart of fresh stock in the fridge.

Who defines abundance, and for whom? Often, people who think like me—who think that having localized agroecology as the foundation of our food consumption is ideal for the environment, our health, our economies, our existence—are considered Luddites or otherwise stuck in the past. It's considered a detriment to really care about how food tastes; this is dismissed as an aesthetic concern. Well, aesthetics matter. Taste matters. Tradition matters. Culture matters. Bones matter, gastronomically and metaphorically. The vegetarian and the vegan: with whom do we align? I know the world I prefer, and it's one where I can have a good-natured ethical argument with someone who cares about their food as much as I do and there are an array of sustainable, ethical, nutritious, accessible choices for those who don't.

Because I don't eat meat, I get a bit emotional about it, sure, but it's also obvious to me how dystopian is any vision of the future that doesn't take into consideration best culinary practices—if it only seeks the same kind of raw efficiency that's currently killing the planet. A world where more people were able to cook, or were nourished by those in their community who enjoy cooking while they do other work? That is a utopian vision that I would vastly prefer to manifest, not least of all because that vision would have me in the kitchen all day rather than here typing. When I was still watching *A Handmaid's Tale*, that vision of a fundamentalist dystopia, I would think, at least I'd be cooking. No matter how the future goes, I'll be in the kitchen. That's my eternal comfort.

Of course, despite all the boosters asking for a policy "moonshot," as Tom Philpott reported for *Mother Jones*, we're actually a long way from lab meat being any sort of reality.[14] It makes more sense, doesn't it, to fight for factory farming to be regulated and its subsidies cut and for us to form a new world in its wake than to waste more breath and newsprint inches on these companies? Why do our visions for the future have to be centered on meat, lab or animal flesh? Why do they have to be centered on corporations at all? Big Ag, Big Meat, Big Fake Meat, Big Fake Egg. There's so much we can change that would make us less dependent. I believe in a world where people realize they don't need meat at every meal, and it's a world where our basic needs are met. It's a world where we have space to reimagine what we consider abundance: an abundance that acknowledges our urgent need for survival.

I don't think it's a bad thing that my food language is so meat-centric; I just want its centricity to feel like more of a relic. I want a future where the ribs of a kale leaf come to mind more readily than those of a pig. In this future, there would be bones for stock, sure, but not as many. Should our legacy be an earth littered with the bones of chickens whose lives were spent miserably in cages? Or should our legacy be one of less waste, of deep flavor, of care?

The food system could hold us back from ever achieving global warming goals if nothing changes about how we use land and what we eat, which is why all the meatposting and angry reactions to cutting back on beef make me feel sad, frustrated, and ineffectual. (And how much do most food writers have in common with the right wing when it comes to the symbolic function of meat? Why is eating meat with abandon getting a thumbs-up on every point on the political spectrum?) Yet they also remind me to get back to work—cooking my vegetables, baking my vegan cake. I'll keep imagining a different world, one where everyone has fruit overflowing on their table, the leisure to cook their family dinner, the money to purchase ingredients that were grown with care by workers paid a fair wage to do so.

That future is possible, as has been imagined by the hippies at The Farm, by Frances Moore Lappé, by punks and anarchists, by vegans and vegetarians, by fighters for food justice. The narrative is up for the taking. The history, the philosophy, and the cuisine are written down for us to learn from, to form a new world with—an abundant one, a caring one, a delicious one. I'm going to go make some mushroom pate, browning minced mushrooms in olive oil in my cast-iron pan; I'll deglaze them with fino sherry, then spread the finished product on toasted baguette. I'll have a passion fruit or two for dessert. I'm going to hope for better, for more, for everyone.

ACKNOWLEDGMENTS

I wrote this book during the thick of the COVID-19 pandemic, utterly unsure of the future, unsure whether what I was writing could be relevant in such a rapidly changing world. I hope it has been.

I want to thank the authors of all the cookbooks I've referenced here for being the keepers of a maligned way of eating, so that I might regard their cooking with the seriousness I believe it deserves.

I want to thank everyone I have ever interviewed for my podcast and for my work as a food writer, for you have provided the foundation of my analysis.

I want to thank the now-women I met as a teenage girl, who gave me so much inspiration that is present in this book by being themselves and sharing with me: Candice Carr and Merette Taylor. To Kerry Roeder, for being the first person who saw me as I wanted to be seen. To Aimée Ortiz, for becoming and being an amazing friend during this tumultuous writing time. To Layla Schlack and Mayukh Sen, for listening and commiserating every day about the highs and lows of the writing life. To my agent, Jenny Stephens, for believing in me before anyone else did.

To my aunts and uncles (Kathy, Diane, Denise, Mary, Rich, Ray, Gene, and Bob) and cousins (Caitlin, Emma, Bobby, Dylan, Richie, Ryan), thank you for your support, humor, and joy throughout my life and helping me develop a thick skin for mockery.

I want to thank my mother, Leslie Locarni, for absolutely everything—chiefly, the ability to find the funny story in every tiny event.

My sister, Cameron, for turning into a nurturing Cancer every time I am the slightest bit upset. My dad, Brian, for making me good at arguing.

To my husband, Israel, thank you for your love and support and martinis throughout this very difficult process. To Benny, our dog, thank you for being by my side the whole time.

BIBLIOGRAPHY

Adams, Carol J. 2015. *The Sexual Politics of Meat—25th-Anniversary Edition*. New York: Bloomsbury Publishing USA.

———. 2018a. *Protest Kitchen*. Newburyport, MA: Conari Press.

———. 2018b. *Burger*. New York: Bloomsbury Publishing USA.

Allison, Karen Hubert. 1998. *The Vegetarian Compass: New Directions in Vegetarian Cooking*. Boston: Little, Brown.

Beaven, Betsey. 1980. *The Political Palate*. Bridgeport, CT: Sanguinaria Publishing.

———. 1984. *The Second Seasonal Political Palate*. Bridgeport, CT: Sanguinaria Publishing.

Belasco, Warren James. 2006. *Appetite for Change: How the Counterculture Took On the Food Industry*. Ithaca, NY: Cornell University Press.

Berley, Peter. 2000. *The Modern Vegetarian Kitchen*. New York: William Morrow Cookbooks.

Berson, Josh. 2019. *The Meat Question: Animals, Humans, and the Deep History of Food*. Cambridge, MA: MIT Press.

Bonney, Grace, ed. 2018. *Good Company*, no. 2. New York: Artisan Books.

Bourdain, Anthony. 2006. *The Nasty Bits: Collected Varietal Cuts, Usable Trim, Scraps, and Bones*. New York: Bloomsbury Publishing USA.

———. 2011. *Medium Raw: A Bloody Valentine to the World of Food and the People Who Cook*. New York: HarperCollins.

Brotman, Juliano, with Erika Lenkert. 1999. *Raw: The UNcook Book; New Vegetarian Food for Life*. New York: William Morrow Cookbooks.

Brown, Edward Espe. 2011. *The Tassajara Bread Book*. Boston: Shambhala Publications.

Brown, Edward Espe, and Deborah Madison. 1987. *The Greens Cookbook*. Toronto: Bantam Dell Publishing Group.

Calvo, Luz, and Catriona Rueda Esquibel. 2015. *Decolonize Your Diet: Plant-Based Mexican-American Recipes for Health and Healing*. Vancouver: Arsenal Pulp Press.

Carson, Rachel. 2002. *Silent Spring*. First published in 1962. Boston: Houghton Mifflin Harcourt.

Cohen, Amanda. 2012. *Dirt Candy: A Cookbook*. New York: Clarkson Potter.

Estabrook, Barry. 2018. *Tomatoland: How Modern Industrial Agriculture Destroyed Our Most Alluring Fruit*. Kansas City, MO: Andrews McMeel.

Feliz Brueck, Julia. 2017. *Veganism in an Oppressive World: A Vegans-of-Color Community Project*. London: Sanctuary Publishers.

Fitzgerald, Matt. 2014. *Diet Cults: The Surprising Fallacy at the Core of Nutrition Fads and a Guide to Healthy Eating for the Rest of Us*. New York: Pegasus Books.

Freedman, Rory, and Kim Barnouin. 2005. *Skinny Bitch: A No-Nonsense, Tough-Love Guide for Savvy Girls Who Want to Stop Eating Crap and Start Looking Fabulous!* Philadelphia: Running Press.

Goldstein, Joyce. 2013. *Inside the California Food Revolution: Thirty Years That Changed Our Culinary Consciousness*. Berkeley: University of California Press.

Hagler, Louise. 1988. *The New Farm Vegetarian Cookbook*. Summertown, TN: Book Publishing Co.

Harper, A. Breeze, ed. 2010. *Sistah Vegan: Black Female Vegans Speak on Food, Identity, Health, and Society*. New York: Lantern Books.

Headley, Brooks. 2014. *Brooks Headley's Fancy Desserts*. New York: W. W. Norton.

———. 2018. *Superiority Burger Cookbook*. New York: W. W. Norton.

Hippycore Krew. 1990. *Soy, Not "Oi!"* San Francisco: AK Press.

Hoffman, Peter. 2021. *What's Good? A Memoir in Fourteen Ingredients*. New York: Abrams Press.

Katz, Sandor Ellix. 2007. *The Revolution Will Not Be Microwaved: Inside America's Underground Food Movements*. White River Junction, VT: Chelsea Green Publishing.

Katzen, Mollie. 1977. *The Moosewood Cookbook: Recipes from Moosewood Restaurant, Ithaca, New York*. Berkeley, CA: Ten Speed Press.

Kauffman, Jonathan. 2018. *Hippie Food: How Back-to-the-Landers, Longhairs, and Revolutionaries Changed the Way We Eat*. New York: HarperCollins.

Kennedy, Alicia. 2018. "Episode 2: Lagusta Yearwood." *Meatless*. https://itunes.apple.com/podcast/id1392676509.

———. 2019. "Episode 24: Amy Quichiz." *Meatless*. https://itunes.apple.com/podcast/id1392676509.

———. 2020. "A Conversation with Bryant Terry." *From the Desk of Alicia Kennedy*. https://itunes.apple.com/podcast/id1608179074.

———. 2021. "A Conversation with Amanda Cohen." *From the Desk of Alicia Kennedy*. https://itunes.apple.com/podcast/id1608179074.

Kenney, Matthew. 2015. *Cooked Raw: How One Celebrity Chef Risked Everything to Change the Way We Eat*. Reedley, CA: Familius.

Kenney, Matthew, and Sarma Melngailis. 2005. *Raw Food for the Real World: 100 Simple to Sophisticated Recipes*. New York: William Morrow Cookbooks.

King, Samantha, R. Scott Carey, Isabel Macquarrie, Victoria N. Millious, and Elaine M. Power, eds. 2019. *Messy Eating: Conversations on Animals as Food*. New York: Fordham University Press.

Kramer, Sarah, and Tanya Barnard. 1999. *How It All Vegan! Irresistible Recipes for an Animal-Free Diet*. Vancouver: Arsenal Pulp Press.

Lappé, Frances Moore. 2010. *Diet for a Small Planet.* 20th anniversary ed. E-book. New York: Ballantine Books.

Lemke-Santangelo, Gretchen. 2009. *Daughters of Aquarius: Women of the Sixties Counterculture.* Lawrence: University Press of Kansas.

Lohman, Sarah. 2016. *Eight Flavors: The Untold Story of American Cuisine.* New York: Simon and Schuster.

Madison, Deborah. 2014. *The New Vegetarian Cooking for Everyone.* Berkeley, CA: Ten Speed Press.

———. 2021. *An Onion in My Pocket: My Life with Vegetables.* New York: Vintage.

McAthy, Karen. 2017. *The Art of Plant-Based Cheesemaking: How to Craft Real, Cultured, Non-Dairy Cheese.* Urban Homesteader Hacks Series. Gabriola Island, BC: New Society Publishers.

McEachern, Leslie. 2019. *The Angelica Home Kitchen: Recipes and Rabble Rousings from an Organic Vegan Restaurant.* Brattleboro, VT: Echo Point Books & Media.

Miriam, Selma, and Noel Furie. 2007. *The Best of Bloodroot.* Bridgeport, CT: Anomaly Press.

Moskowitz, Isa Chandra. 2005. *Vegan with a Vengeance: Over 150 Delicious, Cheap, Animal-Free Recipes That Rock.* New York: Da Capo Lifelong Books.

———. 2016. *The Superfun Times Vegan Holiday Cookbook: Entertaining for Absolutely Every Occasion.* New York: Little, Brown.

Moskowitz, Isa Chandra, and Terry Hope Romero. 2007. *Veganomicon: The Ultimate Vegan Cookbook.* New York: Da Capo Lifelong Books.

Pellow, David Naguib. 2014. *Total Liberation: The Power and Promise of Animal Rights and the Radical Earth Movement.* Minneapolis: University of Minnesota Press.

Ronnen, Tal. 2009. *The Conscious Cook: Delicious Meatless Recipes That Will Change the Way You Eat.* New York: William Morrow Cookbooks.

Roth, Matthew. 2018. *Magic Bean: The Rise of Soy in America.* Lawrence: University of Kansas Press.

Schinner, Miyoko. 2012. *Artisan Vegan Cheese: From Everyday to Gourmet.* Summertown, TN: Book Publishing Co.

———. 2015. *The Homemade Vegan Pantry: The Art of Making Your Own Staples.* Berkeley, CA: Ten Speed Press.

Schinner, Miyoko Nishimoto. 2001. *The New Now and Zen Epicure: Gourmet Vegan Recipes for the Enlightened Palate.* Summertown, TN: Book Publishing Co.

Shprintzen, Adam D. 2015. *The Vegetarian Crusade: The Rise of an American Reform Movement, 1817–1921.* Chapel Hill: University of North Carolina Press.

Shurtleff, William, and Akiko Aoyagi. 1979. *The Book of Tempeh.* New York: Harper & Row.

———. 2014. *Early History of Soybeans and Soyfoods Worldwide (1900–1923).* E-book. Lafayette, CA: SoyInfo Center.

———. 2022. *History of Tofu and Tofu Products (965 CE–1984).* E-book. Lafayette, CA: SoyInfo Center.

Singer, Peter. 2009. *Animal Liberation: The Definitive Classic of the Animal Movement.* First published in 1975. New York: Harper Perennial Modern Classics.

Specht, Joshua. 2020. *Red Meat Republic: A Hoof-to-Table History of How Beef Changed America.* Princeton, NJ: Princeton University Press.

Stuart, Tristram. 2008. *The Bloodless Revolution: A Cultural History of Vegetarianism; From 1600 to Modern Times.* New York: W. W. Norton.

Terry, Bryant. 2014. *Afro-Vegan: Farm-Fresh African, Caribbean & Southern Flavors Remixed.* Berkeley, CA: Ten Speed Press.

———. 2021. *Black Food: Stories, Art & Recipes from Across the African Diaspora.* Berkeley, CA: 4 Color Books.

Thomas, Anna. 1972. *The Vegetarian Epicure.* New York: Vintage.

Trotter, Charlie. 1996. *Charlie Trotter's Vegetables.* Berkeley, CA: Ten Speed Press.

Trotter, Charlie, Roxanne Klein, and Tim Turner. 2003. *Raw.* Berkeley, CA: Ten Speed Press.

Wise, Timothy A. 2019. *Eating Tomorrow: Agribusiness, Family Farmers, and the Battle for the Future of Food.* New York: New Press.

Yearwood, Lagusta. 2019. *Sweet + Salty: The Art of Vegan Chocolates, Truffles, Caramels, and More from Lagusta's Luscious.* New York: Da Capo Lifelong Books.

Zaraska, Marta. 2016. *Meathooked: The History and Science of Our 2.5-Million -Year Obsession with Meat.* New York: Basic Books.

NOTES

INTRODUCTION

1. UN Intergovernmental Panel on Climate Change (IPCC), "Climate Change Widespread, Rapid, and Intensifying," n.d., https://www.ipcc.ch/2021/08/09/ar6-wg1-20210809-pr/, accessed September 15, 2022.

2. IPCC, *Climate Change and Land*, special report, 2020, https://www.ipcc.ch/srccl, accessed September 15, 2022.

3. "Half of the World's Habitable Land Is Used for Agriculture," Our World in Data, n.d., https://ourworldindata.org/global-land-for-agriculture, accessed September 15, 2022.

4. Carol J. Adams and Matthew Calarco, "Derrida and the Sexual Politics of Meat," in *Meat Culture*, ed. Annie Potts (Leiden: Brill, 2016), 31–53.

5. Yarimar Bonilla, "The Coloniality of Disaster: Race, Empire, and the Temporal Logics of Emergency in Puerto Rico, USA," *Political Geography* 78 (2020): 102181, https://doi.org/10.1016/j.polgeo.2020.102181.

6. Dylan Barth, Amelia Kosciulek, and Mark Abadi, "Mushrooms Used to Be Rare in Syria—but Thousands of Refugees Are Now Relying on Them to Survive," *Business Insider*, January 28, 2020, https://www.businessinsider.com/syria-refugees-mushrooms-civil-war-2020-1.

7. David Neimanis, "Reviving Breadfruit, the Polynesian Staple, Could Nourish People and Fight Climate Change," *Civil Eats*, April 28, 2021, https://civileats.com/2021/04/28/reviving-breadfruit-the-polynesian-staple-could-nourish-people-and-fight-climate-change.

8. Sam Bedford, "How Sarajevo's Brewery Helped People Survive the Seige," *Culture Trip*, December 9, 2017, https://theculturetrip.com/europe/bosnia-herzegovina/articles/how-sarajevos-brewery-helped-people-survive-the-seige, accessed September 15, 2022.

9. Franco Ordoñez, "Trump Signs Order to Beef Up Meat Production After Coronavirus Hits Plants," NPR, April 28, 2020, https://www.npr.org/sections/coronavirus-live-updates/2020/04/28/847432897/trump-plans-to-beef-up-meat-production-after-coronavirus-hits-plants.

10. Samantha Fields, "'Record Levels' of Food Insecurity in the U.S. Because of COVID-19," *Marketplace*, May 22, 2020, https://www.marketplace.org/2020/05/22/record-levels-of-food-insecurity-in-the-u-s-because-of-covid-19.

11. Eleanor Cummins, "America's Obsession with Meat, Explained," *Popular Science*, October 28, 2019, https://www.popsci.com/why-americans-eat-so-much-meat; Christina Sewell, "Removing the Meat Subsidy: Our Cognitive Dissonance Around Animal Agriculture," *Journal of International Affairs*, February 10, 2020, https://jia.sipa.columbia.edu/removing-meat-subsidy-our-cognitive-dissonance-around-animal-agriculture.

12. Hannah Ritchie, "Half of the World's Habitable Land Is Used for Agriculture," Our World in Data, November 11, 2019, https://ourworldindata.org/global-land-for-agriculture, accessed September 15, 2022.

13. John Holmes, "Losing 25,000 to Hunger Every Day," *UN Chronicle* 45, no. 3 (2009): 14–20, https://doi.org/10.18356/a54cdeod-en.

14. Berson, *The Meat Question*.

CHAPTER ONE: DIET FOR WHOSE PLANET?

1. Lappé, *Diet for a Small Planet*.

2. Kauffman, *Hippie Food*.

3. Shprintzen, *The Vegetarian Crusade*.

4. "A Conversation with Bryant Terry," *From the Desk of Alicia Kennedy*, May 29, 2020, https://www.aliciakennedy.news/p/5292020-a-conversation-with-bryant.

5. Malcolm X, "Afro-American History (January 1964)," https://www.marxists.org/reference/archive/malcolm-x/1965/01/afro-amer.html.

6. Althea Smith, "A Farewell to Chitterlings: Vegetarianism Is on the Rise Among Diet-Conscious Blacks," *Ebony*, September 1974.

7. Jennifer Jensen Wallach, *How to Eat to Live: Black Nationalism and the Post-1964 Culinary Turn*, Center for the Study of Southern Culture, University of Mississippi, July 2014, https://southernstudies.olemiss.edu/study-the-south/how-to-eat-to-live.

8. Wallach, *How to Eat to Live*.

9. Amirah Mercer, "A Homecoming," *Eater*, January 14, 2021, https://www.eater.com/22229322/black-veganism-history-black-panthers-dick-gregory-nation-of-islam-alvenia-fulton.

10. Clarissa Wei, "Not Impossible: China's Rich Vegan Meat Culture Goes Back 1,000 Years," *Goldthread*, June 15, 2020, https://www.goldthread2.com/food/chinese-fake-meat/article/3089139.

11. Stuart, *The Bloodless Revolution*.

12. Lisa Betty, "Veganism* Is in Crisis—as an Anti-Oppressive Social (Justice) Movement," *Medium*, December 6, 2021, https://lbetty1.medium.com/veganism-is-in-crisis-36f78fa9a4b9.

13. Kennedy, "Episode 24: Amy Quichiz."

14. Joanna Blythman, "Can Vegans Stomach the Unpalatable Truth About Quinoa?" *The Guardian*, January 16, 2013, https://www.theguardian.com/commentisfree/2013/jan/16/vegans-stomach-unpalatable-truth-quinoa.

15. "The Nutrition Transition," Obesity Prevention Source, Harvard T. H. Chan School of Public Health, https://www.hsph.harvard.edu/obesity-prevention-source/nutrition-transition, accessed September 15, 2022.

16. Fumiaki Imamura et al., "Dietary Quality Among Men and Women in 187 Countries in 1990 and 2010: A Systematic Assessment," *The Lancet* 3, no. 3 (2015), https://www.thelancet.com/journals/langlo/article/PIIS2214-109 X(14)70381-X/fulltext.

17. Organisation for Economic Co-operation Development and the Food and Agricultural Organization, *OECD-FAO Agricultural Outlook 2021–2030*, "Chapter 6: Meat," https://www.fao.org/3/cb5332en/Meat.pdf.

18. Calvo and Esquibel, *Decolonize Your Diet*.

19. Margaret Robinson, "Veganism and Mi'kmaq Legends," in *Meatsplaining: The Animal Agriculture Industry and the Rhetoric of Denial*, ed. Jason Hannan (Sydney: Sydney University Press, 2020).

20. IPCC, *Climate Change and Land*, special report, "Technical Summary," 2020, https://www.ipcc.ch/site/assets/uploads/sites/4/2022/11/SRCCL _Technical-Summary.pdf.

21. IPCC, *Climate Change and Land*, "Chapter 5: Food Security," 2020, https://www.ipcc.ch/srccl/chapter/chapter-5, accessed September 15, 2022.

22. Tamar Haspel, Twitter post, January 3, 2022, 11:24 a.m., https:// twitter.com/TamarHaspel/status/1478024481792737280.

23. Kenny Torrella, "The Environmental Limits of Eating Local," *Vox*, June 6, 2022, https://www.vox.com/future-perfect/23132579/eat-local-csa -farmers-markets-locavore-slow-food; Philip Maughan, "Against Localism in Food," *Noema*, September 7, 2022, https://www.noemamag.com/against -localism-in-food.

24. Dan Charles, "How Puerto Rico Lost Its Home-Grown Food, but Might Find It Again," NPR, May 13, 2017, https://www.npr.org/sections /thesalt/2017/05/13/527934047/how-puerto-rico-lost-its-home-grown-food -but-might-find-it-again.

25. LinYee Yuan, "Seed Freedom: Toward an Earth Democracy; a Conversation with Vandana Shiva," *Mold*, November 9, 2021, https://thisismold .com/mold-magazine/vandana-shiva-seed-freedom-toward-an-earth -democracy.

26. Lisa Elaine Held, "In the Midst of a Climate Crisis, Does Local Food Matter?" *Peeled*, July 8, 2021, https://peeled.substack.com/p/in-the-midst-of -a-climate-crisis.

27. Henry I. Miller and Jayson Lusk, "Beware the High Priests of Locavorism," Hoover Institution, April 18, 2013, https://www.hoover.org/research /beware-high-priests-locavorism, accessed October 24, 2022.

28. Christina Sewell, "Removing the Meat Subsidy: Our Cognitive Dissonance Around Animal Agriculture," *Journal of International Affairs*, February 11, 2020, https://jia.sipa.columbia.edu/removing-meat-subsidy-our-cognitive -dissonance-around-animal-agriculture.

29. Sky Chadde, "COVID-19 Cases, Death in Meatpacking Industry Were Much Higher Than Previously Known, Congressional Investigation Shows," Investigate Midwest, October 28, 2021, https://investigatemidwest .org/2021/10/28/covid-19-cases-deaths-in-meatpacking-industry-were-much -higher-than-previously-known-congressional-investigation-shows.

CHAPTER TWO: MEAT'S MEANING

1. Nina Lakhani, "'They Rake in Profits—Everyone Else Suffers': US Workers Lose Out as Big Chicken Gets Bigger," *The Guardian*, August 11, 2022, https://www.theguardian.com/environment/2021/aug/11/tyson-chicken -indsutry-arkansas-poultry-monopoly.

2. Stephen Groves and Stephanie Tareen, "Worker Shortage Concerns Loom in Immigrant-Heavy Meatpacking," Associated Press, May 25, 2020, https://apnews.com/article/south-dakota-ne-state-wire-us-news-ap-top-news -virus-outbreak-db42b45724befc83b2371450f149c711.

3. Alice Driver, "Their Lives on the Line," *New York Review of Books*, April 27, 2021, https://www.nybooks.com/daily/2021/04/27/their-lives-on-the-line.

4. Human Rights Watch, *"When We're Dead and Buried, Our Bones Will Keep Hurting": Workers' Rights Under Threat in US Meat and Poultry Plants*, 2019, https://www.hrw.org/sites/default/files/report_pdf/us0919_web.pdf.

5. Allen Smith, "House Subcommittee: Nearly 60,000 Meatpacking Workers Got COVID-19," Society for Human Resource Management, October 29, 2021, https://www.shrm.org/resourcesandtools/legal-and-compliance /employment-law/pages/coronavirus-house-subcommittee-meatpacking -workers.aspx.

6. Alex Shephard, "How the *Daily Mail* Is Feeding the Right-Wing Culture War," *New Republic*, April 27, 2021, https://newrepublic.com/article /162187/daily-mail-feeding-right-wing-culture-war.

7. Jaclyn Krymowski, "The Story Behind Agriculture's Commodity Checkoff Programs," *AGDAILY*, October 21, 2020, https://www.agdaily.com /insights/history-behind-agricultures-commodity-checkoff-programs.

8. Dan Bobkoff, "What Elevated Kale from Vegetable to Cultural Identifier?" NPR, September 5, 2013, https://www.npr.org/2013/09/05/219368062 /what-elevated-kale-from-vegetable-to-cultural-identifier.

9. Rebekah Kebede, "Who Owns Kale?" *National Geographic*, August 10, 2016, https://www.nationalgeographic.com/culture/article/who-owns-kale-.

10. Specht, *Red Meat Republic*.

11. "Per Capita Meat Consumption in the United States in 2020 and 2030, by Type (in Pounds)," Statista, 2021, https://www.statista.com/statistics /189222/average-meat-consumption-in-the-us-by-sort.

12. Leah Garces, "Replacing Beef with Chicken Isn't As Good for the Planet As You Think," *Vox*, December 4, 2019, https://www.vox.com/future-perfect /2019/12/4/20993654/chicken-beef-climate-environment-factory-farms.

13. IFT, "Global Meat Consumption Continues to Rise," March 2, 2020, https://www.ift.org/news-and-publications/news/2020/march/02/global-meat -consumption-continues-to-rise; Tony McDougal, "Poultry Poised to Take Nearly Half of the Global Meat Market by 2031," *Poultry World*, July 29, 2022, https://www.poultryworld.net/the-industrymarkets/market-trends-analysis-the -industrymarkets-2/poultry-set-to-take-nearly-half-of-the-global-meat-market -by-2031.

14. Max Pearl, Twitter post, February 23, 2021, 4:16 p.m., https://twitter .com/maxpearl/status/1364308154117476356?s=20&t=dyM-7vrfezqsBB 18pkn4Pw.

15. Alicia Kennedy to Andrea Aliseda, emails "Re: Vegan al Pastor," March 2, 2021.

16. Jan Dutkiewicz and Gabriel N. Rosenberg, "The Sadism of Eating Real Meat over Lab Meat," *New Republic*, February 23, 2021, https://newrepublic .com/article/161452/sadism-eating-real-meat-lab-meat.

17. Tim Carman, "Burger King's Impossible Whopper Is Going National. Is That Bad News for Small Restaurants?" *Washington Post*, April 29, 2019, https://www.washingtonpost.com/news/voraciously/wp/2019/04/29/burger -kings-impossible-whopper-is-going-national-is-that-bad-news-for-small -restaurants.

18. Tad Friend, "Can a Burger Help Solve Climate Change?" *New Yorker*, September 23, 2019, https://www.newyorker.com/magazine/2019/09/30/can-a -burger-help-solve-climate-change.

19. Berson, *The Meat Question*.

20. Impossible Foods, "Impossible™ Burger Debuts in 200 Asian Grocery Stores," press release, October 19, 2020, https://impossiblefoods.com/media /news-releases/2020/10/impossible-foods-accelerates-international-growth -as-flagship-product-debuts-in-asian-grocery-stores.

21. Reuters Staff, "Plant-Based Egg Producer Eat Just to Build Singapore Factory," Reuters, October 20, 2020, https://www.reuters.com/article/us-eat -just-singapore-idUSKBN2750YC.

22. Megan Poinski, "Aleph Farms Unveils World's First Cell-Based Rib-eye Steak," *FoodDive*, February 1, 2020, https://www.fooddive.com/news/aleph -farms-unveils-worlds-first-cell-based-ribeye-steak/594830.

23. Emma Newburger and Amelia Lucas, "Beyond Meat Uses Climate Change to Market Fake Meat Substitutes. Scientists Are Cautious," CNBC, September 2, 2019, https://www.cnbc.com/2019/09/02/beyond-meat-uses -climate-change-to-market-fake-meat-substitutes-scientists-are-cautious.html.

24. John Lynch and Raymond Pierrehumbert, "Climate Impacts of Cultured Meat and Beef Cattle," *Frontiers in Sustainable Food Systems*, February 2019, https://www.frontiersin.org/articles/10.3389/fsufs.2019.00005/full.

25. Zaraska, *Meathooked*.

26. Marta Zaraska to Alicia Kennedy, email, April 12, 2016.

27. Mike Murphy, "Beyond Meat Soars 163% in Biggest-Popping U.S. IPO Since 2000," *MarketWatch*, May 2, 2019, https://www.marketwatch.com /story/beyond-meat-soars-163-in-biggest-popping-us-ipo-since-2000-2019 -05-02.

28. Emiko Terazono, "Beyond Meat Takes a Beating as Plant-Based Sector Reports Slowing Sales," *Financial Times*, February 25, 2022, https://www.ft .com/content/9ccf053a-e710-462f-9a8e-1ddodb13a523.

29. Bloomberg, "Burger King Cuts Impossible Whopper Price as Sales Slow," *Los Angeles Times*, January 22, 2020, https://www.latimes.com/business /story/2020-01-22/burger-king-cuts-impossible-whopper-price-as-sales-slow; Leslie Patton and Deena Shanker, "Faux Meat Falters at the Drive-Thru," *Bloomberg*, September 24, 2021, https://www.bloomberg.com/news/articles /2021-09-24/which-fast-food-has-fake-meat-not-many-serve-beyond-meat -impossible-foods.

30. "OECD-FAO Agricultural Outlook 2021–2030," *Meat* (2021): 163–77, https://doi.org/10.1787/74b9be71-en.

CHAPTER THREE: FOUNDATIONS OF A NEW AMERICAN CUISINE
1. "USDA Coexistence Fact Sheets: Soybeans," USDA, February 2015, https://www.usda.gov/sites/default/files/documents/coexistence-soybeans -factsheet.pdf.
2. "GMO Crops in the U.S.," FDA, July 2022, https://www.fda.gov /media/135274/download#:~:text=It%20is%20also%20used%20as,7%20of %20all%20soybeans%20planted; Mark Messina, "Prevalence of Soy Allergy Lowest Among the Big 8," Soy Nutrition Institute, February 4, 2020, https:// thesoynutritioninstitute.com/prevalence-of-soy-allergy-lowest-among-the -big-8.
3. William Shurtleff, "Chronology of Tofu Worldwide," SoyInfo Center, 2001, https://www.soyinfocenter.com/chronologies_of_soyfoods-tofu.php.
4. Akiko Aoyagi and William Shurtleff, *History of Seitan (1962–2022)* (La-fayette, CA: SoyInfo Center, 2022), https://www.soyinfocenter.com/pdf/277 /Seit.pdf.
5. "The Plowboy Interview: Bill Shurtleff and Akiko Aoyagi," *Mother Earth News*, March 1, 1977, https://www.motherearthnews.com/real-food /akiko-aoyagi-zmaz77mazbon.
6. Kate Bratskeir, "Soy Boys: How Tofu Conquered the Supermarket During a Global Pandemic," *Inverse*, March 24, 2021, https://www.inverse .com/culture/history-of-tofu-america-pandemic.
7. Fred Yi, "Seventh-Day Adventists and Health," PBS, March 23, 2012, https://www.pbs.org/wnet/religionandethics/2012/03/23/march-23-2012 -seventh-day-adventists-and-health/10575.
8. William Shurtleff, *History of Soy Ice Cream and Other Non-Dairy Frozen Desserts (1899–2013)* (Lafayette, CA: SoyInfo Center, 2013), https://www.soy infocenter.com/books/167; William Shurtleff, *History of Meat Alternatives (965 CE to 2014)* (Lafayette, CA: SoyInfo Center, 2014), https://www.soyinfocenter .com/pdf/179/MAL.pdf.
9. Nadia Berenstein, "A History of Soy Milk," *Serious Eats*, November 6, 2019, https://www.seriouseats.com/a-brief-history-of-soy-milk-the-future -food-of-yesterday#:~:text=After%20hitting%20a%20peak%20of,of%20 %24300%20million%20in%202015.
10. Kate Knibbs, "The Alt-Right's Newest Insult: Soy Boy," *The Ringer*, November 3, 2017, https://www.theringer.com/tech/2017/11/3/16598872 /alt-right-lingo-soy-boy.
11. William Shurtleff, "Recent History of Soy in Cuba," SoyInfo Center, January 1996, https://www.soyinfocenter.com/HSS/recent-history-of-soy-in -cuba.php.
12. Ina Ghita, "Altering Cooking and Eating Habits During the Romanian Communist Regime by Using Cookbooks: A Digital History Project," *Encounters in Theory and History of Education* 19 (2018): 141–62, http://doi.dx.org /10.24908/eoe-ese-rse.v19i0.6752.

13. Esther Sung, "Q&A with Mollie Katzen," Epicurious, 2013, https://www.epicurious.com/archive/chefsexperts/interviews/mollie-katzen-moose wood-vegetarian-qa-recipes, accessed October 24, 2022.

14. Nora Ephron, "The Food Establishment," in *American Food Writing: An Anthology with Classic Recipes*, ed. Molly O'Neill (New York: Library of America, 2007).

15. Gregory Dicum, "Expanding the Frontiers of the Vegetarian Plate," *New York Times*, November 18, 2007, https://www.nytimes.com/2007/11/18/travel/18Choice.html.

16. Ruth Reichl, "The Most Interesting Piece I Ever Wrote?" (1979), reprinted in *La Briffe*, December 2, 2021, https://ruthreichl.substack.com/p/dec-2-template.

17. Goldstein, *Inside the California Food Revolution*.

18. Eric Asimov, "It's Easier to Be Green," *New York Times*, April 8, 2001, https://www.nytimes.com/2001/04/08/weekinreview/it-s-easier-to-be-green.html.

19. Larissa Zimberoff, "Tofu Goes Mainstream in America Thanks to Big Meat's Covid Crisis," *Bloomberg*, June 11, 2020, https://www.bloomberg.com/news/articles/2020-06-11/the-pandemic-opens-the-door-to-tofu-makers-who-race-to-meet-deman.

20. Amanda Cohen, author interviews, 2019–2022.

CHAPTER FOUR: TOWARD A POLITICAL PALATE

1. Max Berlinger, "How Erewhon Became L.A.'s Hottest Hangout," *New York Times*, February 17, 2021, https://www.nytimes.com/2021/02/17/style/erewhon-los-angeles-health-food.html.

2. Kevin Kelly, "Why We Left the Farm," *Whole Earth Review*, Winter 1985, available at https://kk.org/mt-files/writings/why_we_left_the_farm.pdf.

3. Stephanie Hartman, "The Political Palate: Reading Commune Cookbooks," *Gastronomica* 3, no. 2 (Spring 2003): 29–40, https://doi.org/10.1525/gfc.2003.3.2.29.

4. Lemke-Santangelo, *Daughters of Aquarius*.

5. This section is based on Alicia Kennedy, "This Consciousness-Raising Cafe Wants You to Eat Like a Feminist," *Vice*, February 7, 2018, https://www.vice.com/en/article/mgxkd3/this-consciousness-raising-cafe-wants-you-to-eat-like-a-feminist.

6. Greta Gaard, "Ecofeminism Revisited: Rejecting Essentialism and Re-Placing Species in a Material Feminist Environmentalism," *Feminist Formations* 23, no. 2 (Summer 2011): 26–53, https://doi.org/10.2307/41301655.

7. Alexandra (Alex) Diva Ketchum, "Serving Up Revolution: Feminist Restaurants, Cafés, and Coffeehouses in the United States and Canada from 1972 to 1989," diss., McGill University, 2018.

8. Deborah Madison, "Deborah Madison Is Done with Cookbooks. Now, She's Making Corn Dogs and Fried Chicken," *The Counter*, June 30, 2021, https://thecounter.org/rewrites-deborah-madison-retirement-pandemic-vegetarian-cooking-meat.

CHAPTER FIVE: PUNK GOES MAINSTREAM (SORT OF)

1. Penelope Green, "Anarchy Rules: The Dishes Stay Dirty," *New York Times*, January 3, 2008, https://www.nytimes.com/2008/01/03/garden/03 punk.html.

2. Hippycore Krew, *Soy, Not "Oi!,"* edited and with an introduction by Joel Olson (Oakland, CA: AK Press, 2005).

3. André Gallant, "Seasoned Punks: An Education in Cast Iron from the South's Greatest Unknown Punk Trio," *Southern Cultures* 24, no. 2 (2018): 51–59, doi:10.1353/scu.2018.0019.

4. Peter Gelderloos, "Veganism: Why Not, an Anarchist Perspective," Anarchist Library, 2011, https://theanarchistlibrary.org/library/peter-gelderloos -veganism-why-not.

5. The section on zines borrows from Alicia Kennedy, "How Zines Became an Anarchist's Guide to Cooking Vegan," *Nylon*, https://www.nylon.com /vegan-zines-recipes-brownies, accessed December 9, 2022.

6. The section on Yearwood borrows from Alicia Kennedy, "Lagusta Yearwood, the Punk Chocolatier," *The Hairpin*, January 14, 2015, https://www .thehairpin.com/2015/01/lagusta-yearwood-the-punk-chocolatier; the *Good Company* citation is for issue 2: The Fear(less) Issue, October 2018.

7. Various interviews with the author, 2014–18.

CHAPTER SIX: MEATLESS PLURALITY

1. Matthew Scully, "Building a Better State of the Union Address," opinion, *New York Times*, February 2, 2005, https://www.nytimes.com/2005/02/02 /opinion/building-a-better-state-of-the-union-address.html; "Costs of War: Iraqi Civilians," Watson Institute of International and Public Affairs, Brown University, June 2021, https://watson.brown.edu/costsofwar/costs/human /civilians/iraqi.

2. Tammy La, "Conservative and a Vegan in New York. Wait! You Are, Too?" *New York Times*, July 20, 2018, https://www.nytimes.com/2018/07/20 /fashion/weddings/two-unhip-conservative-vegans-in-new-york-marry.html.

3. Sarah Manavis, "Eco-Fascism: The Ideology Marrying Environmentalism and White Supremacy Thriving Online," *New Statesman*, September 21, 2018, https://www.newstatesman.com/science-tech/2018/09/eco-fascism -ideology-marrying-environmentalism-and-white-supremacy.

4. Frances Moore Lappé and Rachel Schurman, "The Missing Piece in the Population Puzzle," Food First, September 1, 1988, https://archive.foodfirst .org/publication/the-missing-piece-in-the-population-puzzel.

5. "What Is Food Justice?" FoodPrint, published October 8, 2018, last updated March 11, 2021, https://foodprint.org/issues/food-justice.

6. "Where Is the Diversity in Publishing? The 2019 Diversity Baseline Survey Results," *Lee & Low* (blog), January 28, 2020, https://blog.leeandlow .com/2020/01/28/2019diversitybaselinesurvey.

7. Julia Turshen, "To Change Racial Disparity in Food, Let's Start with Cookbooks," *Eater*, April 5, 2018, https://www.eater.com/2018/4/5/17153806 /racial-inequality-food-cookbook-authors-publishing.

8. Elizabeth A. Harris and Concepción de León, "Black Chefs Are Landing More Cookbook Deals. Is That Enough?" *New York Times*, August 24, 2020, https://www.nytimes.com/2020/08/24/books/black-food-writers-cookbook-publishing.html.

9. Lauren Collins, "Alison Roman Just Can't Help Herself," *New Yorker*, December 13, 2021, https://www.newyorker.com/magazine/2021/12/20/alison-roman-just-cant-help-herself.

10. Anna Lappé and Bryant Terry, *Grub: Ideas for an Urban Organic Kitchen* (New York: Tarcher/Penguin, 2006).

11. Ashanté M. Reese, "A Review of 'By Any Greens Necessary: A Revolutionary Guide for Black Women Who Want to Eat Great, Get Healthy, Lose Weight, and Look Phat'; 'Sistah Vegan: Black Female Vegans Speak on Food, Identity, Health, and Society,'" *Food and Foodways* 22 (3): 217–21, https://doi.org/10.1080/07409710.2014.931684.

12. Harper, *Sistah Vegan*.

13. Robinson, "Veganism and Mi'kmaq Legends."

14. Kim Severson, "Black Vegans Step Out, for Their Health and Other Causes," *New York Times*, November 28, 2017, https://www.nytimes.com/2017/11/28/dining/black-vegan-cooking.html.

CHAPTER SEVEN: WHEATGRASS AND WELLNESS

1. Nina Mackert and Friedrich Schorb, "Introduction to the Special Issue: Public Health, Healthism, and Fatness," *Fat Studies* 11, no. 1 (2022): 1–7, https://www.tandfonline.com/doi/full/10.1080/21604851.2021.1911486.

2. Corey Lee Wrenn, "Fat Vegan Politics: A Survey of Fat Vegan Activists' Online Experiences with Social Movement Sizeism," *Fat Studies* 6, no. 1 (2017): 90–102.

3. Laura Wright, *The Vegan Studies Project: Food, Animals, and Gender in the Age of Terror* (Athens: University of Georgia Press, 2015), 105.

4. Victoria Moran, "Unsung Heroes," *Vegetarian Times*, December 1990.

5. "Florida 'Doctor' Who Treated Aboriginal Girls with Leukemia Ordered to 'Cease and Desist,'" CBC, February 24, 2015, https://www.cbc.ca/news/indigenous/brian-clement-hippocrates-health-institute-head-ordered-to-stop-practising-medicine-1.2968780.

6. Michael Bauer, "Dining Out: Something New Isn't Cooking Here / Raw Living Foods in the Sunset Specializes in Natural, Unheated Nourishment," *San Francisco Chronicle*, December 17, 1995, https://www.sfchronicle.com/restaurants/diningout/article/DINING-OUT-Something-New-Isn-t-Cooking-Here-3018128.php.

7. Laura Reiley, "Raw Ambition," *Tampa Bay Times*, June 8, 2008, https://www.tampabay.com/archive/2008/06/08/raw-ambition.

8. Kim Severson, "Shangri-La in the Raw: Pioneering Marin Chef Breaks a Culinary Barrier," *SFGate*, April 17, 2002, https://www.sfgate.com/recipes/article/Shangri-la-in-the-raw-Pioneering-Marin-chef-2851140.php.

9. Madeline Stone, "An Entrepreneur Has Sold San Francisco's Most Expensive Home for $31 Million," *Business Insider*, May 18, 2015, https://www

.businessinsider.com/entrepreneur-sells-most-expensive-home-in-san-francisco
-2015-5.

10. Russell Scott Smith, "Onan the Vegetarian: A Raw-Food Guru Turns 'Subway Perv,'" *New York*, March 30, 2006, https://nymag.com/news/features /16576.

11. Serena Dai, "Raw Food Star Sarma Melngailis Finally Arrested After Disappearing During Wage Lawsuit," *Eater NY*, May 12, 2016, https://ny .eater.com/2016/5/12/11663502/sarma-melngailis-arrested.

CHAPTER EIGHT: NON-DAIRY DAIRY

1. Matt Hale, "Exploring the Growth of Plant-Based Milk," *Food Manufacturing*, September 23, 2021, https://www.foodmanufacturing.com/consumer -trends/article/21723117/exploring-the-growth-of-plantbased-milk.

2. "Environmental Impacts of Food Production," Our World in Data, https://ourworldindata.org/environmental-impacts-of-food, accessed September 15, 2022.

3. "Definition & Facts for Lactose Intolerance," National Institute of Diabetes and Digestive and Kidney Diseases, February 2018, https://www.niddk .nih.gov/health-information/digestive-diseases/lactose-intolerance/definition -facts.

4. William Shurtleff and Akiko Aoyagi, *History of Soybeans and Soyfoods in France (1665–2015)* (Lafayette, CA: SoyInfo Center, 2015).

5. This section borrows from Alicia Kennedy, "Vegan Cheese Is Ready to Compete with Dairy. Is the World Ready to Eat It?" *Eater*, April 1, 2021, https://www.eater.com/22315684/vegan-cheese-history-ingredients-process -grocery-brands.

6. Grand View Research, *Vegan Cheese Market Size, Share & Trends Analysis Report by Product (Mozzarella, Ricotta, Cheddar, Parmesan, Cream Cheese), by Source (Cashew, Soy), by End Use (B2C, B2B), by Region, and Segment Forecasts, 2022–2030*, Report ID: GVR-4-68039-024-2, https://www.grandviewresearch .com/industry-analysis/vegan-cheese-market.

7. Allee Manning, "Häagen-Dazs Just Answered Your Dairy-Free Prayers," *Self*, July 6, 2017, https://www.self.com/story/dairy-free-haagen-dazs.

8. Erica M. Schulte et al., "Which Foods May Be Addictive? The Roles of Processing, Fat Content, and Glycemic Load," *PLoS One* 10, no. 2 (February 2018): e0117959, https://pubmed.ncbi.nlm.nih.gov/25692302; Jenn Harris, "Cheese Really Is Crack. Study Reveals Cheese Is as Addictive as Drugs," *Los Angeles Times*, October 22, 2015, https://www.latimes.com/food/dailydish/la -dd-cheese-addictive-drugs-20151022-story.html.

9. Anthony Schneck, "Dairy Crack: The Science Behind Your Crippling Cheese Addiction," *Thrillist*, October 8, 2015, https://www.thrillist.com/health /nation/why-cheese-is-so-addictive.

10. Tara Duggan, "Vegan Cheese Startup Miyoko's Kitchen Drawing Lots of Investors," *SFGate*, February 15, 2017, https://www.sfgate.com/business /article/Vegan-cheese-company-draws-big-bucks-from-startup-10935279.php.

11. Civil Eats Editors, "Civil Eats TV: Meet the Queen of Vegan Cheese," *Civil Eats*, September 1, 2020, https://civileats.com/2020/09/01/civil-eats-tv -meet-the-queen-of-vegan-cheese.

12. Elaine Watson, "Lawsuit vs. Miyoko's Kitchen Challenging Plant-Based 'Butter' Is Voluntarily Dismissed," *Food Navigator*, May 17, 2019, https://www.foodnavigator-usa.com/Article/2019/05/17/Lawsuit-vs-Miyoko -s-Kitchen-challenging-plant-based-butter-is-voluntarily-dismissed#.

13. Joe Fassler, "After Backing Out of Beyond Meat, Tyson Foods Announces a New Plant-Based Brand of Its Own," *The Counter*, June 13, 2019, https://thecounter.org/after-backing-out-of-beyond-meat-tyson-foods -announces-a-new-plant-based-brand-of-its-own/; Elaine Watson, "Chobani Goes Beyond Dairy: 'For Some Time, We've Felt That People Deserve Better Non-Dairy Options,'" *Food Navigator*, March 14, 2019, https://www.food navigator-usa.com/Article/2019/01/09/Chobani-unveils-plant-based-yogurt -For-some-time-we-ve-felt-that-people-deserve-better-non-dairy-options.

14. Anna Starostinetskaya, "Dairy Brand Boursin Launches Vegan Cheese Spread," *VegNews*, October 13, 2020, https://vegnews.com/2020/10/dairy -brand-boursin-launches-vegan-cream-cheese.

15. Catherine Lamb, "FDA Approves Perfect Day's Animal-Free Whey Protein as Safe to Eat," *The Spoon*, April 15, 2020, https://thespoon.tech/fda -approves-perfect-days-animal-free-whey-protein-as-safe-to-eat.

16. Richard Bowie, "Starbucks Is Now Testing Vegan Miyoko's Cream Cheese," *VegNews*, September 20, 2020, https://vegnews.com/2020/9/starbucks -is-now-testing-vegan-miyoko-s-cream-cheese.

17. Eric Pfanner, "Starbucks Says Hold the Milk to Reduce Carbon Footprint," *Bloomberg*, January 21, 2020, https://www.bloomberg.com/news /articles/2020-01-21/starbucks-says-hold-the-milk-as-it-moves-to-cut-carbon -footprint?srnd=green.

18. Chloe Sorvino, "Lifeless Market for Meatless Meat," *Forbes*, June 18, 2022, https://www.forbes.com/sites/chloesorvino/2022/06/18/lifeless-market -for-meatless-meat/?sh=494f34498f24.

19. Summer Anne Burton, "I Ate Pizza Hut's New Vegan Pizza and Now I'm Here to Tell You About It," *Tenderly*, November 20, 2020, https://tenderly .medium.com/i-ate-pizza-huts-new-vegan-pizza-and-now-i-m-here-to-tell -you-about-it-4940530deo6d.

20. Edward Helmore, "Activists Sour on Oatly Vegan Milk After Stake Sold to Trump-Linked Blackstone," *The Guardian*, September 2, 2020, https:// www.theguardian.com/food/2020/sep/01/oatly-vegan-milk-sale-blackstone.

CHAPTER NINE: THE FUTURE OF FOOD

1. Joe Fassler, "Lab-Grown Meat Is Supposed to Be Inevitable. The Science Tells a Different Story," *The Counter*, September 22, 2021, https:// thecounter.org/lab-grown-cultivated-meat-cost-at-scale.

2. Charlie Mitchell, "Fake Meat, Real Profits," *The Baffler*, January 27, 2021, https://thebaffler.com/latest/fake-meat-real-profits-mitchell.

3. Michele Simon, "Opinion: Are Vegan Meat Alternatives Really Saving Animals?" *VegNews*, August 6, 2021, https://vegnews.com/2021/8/vegan-meat-alternatives-saving-animals.

4. Michele Simon, "5 Lessons Cell Cultured Meat Companies Can Learn from the Theranos Verdict," *Forbes*, January 6, 2022, https://www.forbes.com/sites/michelesimon/2022/01/06/5-lessons-cell-cultured-meat-companies-can-learn-from-the-theranos-verdict/?sh=46c8ab521947.

5. Britt H. Young, "Incubated Futures," *N+1*, September 16, 2022, https://www.nplusonemag.com/online-only/online-only/incubated-futures.

6. Wise, *Eating Tomorrow*.

7. Kara Swisher, "Innovation, Not Trees. How Bill Gates Plans to Save the Planet," *New York Times*, February 15, 2021, https://www.nytimes.com/2021/02/15/opinion/sway-kara-swisher-bill-gates.html.

8. "Texas Freeze Delivers Billions in Profits to Gas and Power Sellers," Reuters, May 6, 2021, https://www.reuters.com/business/energy/results-tally-up-billions-profit-texas-freeze-gas-power-sellers-2021-05-06.

9. Terry Nguyen, "In Crisis, Texans Are Turning Toward Mutual Aid Networks," *Vox*, February 18, 2021, https://www.vox.com/the-goods/22289581/mutual-aid-helps-texas-storm.

10. Ligaya Mishan, "The Activists Working to Remake the Food System," *T: The New York Times Style Magazine*, February 19, 2021, https://www.nytimes.com/2021/02/19/t-magazine/food-security-activists.html.

11. Alexandria Ocasio-Cortez, Twitter post, February 17, 2021, 12:26 p.m., https://twitter.com/AOC/status/1362075902541201409?s=20&t=zI2MeukICTrqjKESRiYL8A.

12. Chris Casey, "Biden Gives Small Meat Processors $1B to Support Competition," *FoodDive*, January 4, 2022, https://www.fooddive.com/news/biden-gives-small-meat-processors-1b-to-support-competition/616622.

13. Pete Wells, "Eleven Madison Park Explores the Plant Kingdom's Uncanny Valley," *New York Times*, September 28, 2021, updated October 1, 2021, https://www.nytimes.com/2021/09/28/dining/eleven-madison-park-restaurant-review-plant-based.html.

14. Tom Philpott, "Is Lab Meat About to Hit Your Dinner Plate?" *Mother Jones*, August 2, 2021, https://www.motherjones.com/food/2021/08/is-lab-meat-about-to-hit-your-dinner-plate.

INDEX